The Slaves Shall Serve
Meditations on Liberty

THE SLAVES SHALL SERVE

MEDITATIONS ON LIBERTY

JAMES WASSERMAN

SEKMET BOOKS
NEW YORK

First Edition Published 2004 by
SEKMET BOOKS
A division of Studio 31, Inc.
Visit our website: www.sekmetbooks.com

For orders and sales information, please email: info@sekmetbooks.com

STUDIO 31, INC.
P.O. Box 33
Peter Stuyvesant Station
New York, NY 10009
www.studio31.com

ISBN: 0-9718870-1-2

Library of Congress Cataloging-in-publication data available

Book design and typography by STUDIO 31

Cover art by permission: Scala/Art Resource, NY
The Expulsion from the Garden of Eden (1425–28) by Masaccio (1401–28)
Brancacci Chapel, Florence, Italy (Pre-Restoration)

Printed in the U.S.A. on acid free paper

Those who beat their swords into plowshares

Will do the plowing for those who don't.

This book is dedicated to

Those who Won't.

ACKNOWLEDGMENTS

Once again, I begin by thanking my wife, Nancy. This book emerged from a great deal of pain that, I suspect, at times may have been worse for her. She stood by me as I learned to regain my courage and sense of humor.

Certain friends have been especially valued companions on this journey. I think of Richard Capuro, Anthony Carlson, Michael Kramer, Richard Wenzler, David Lewis, Alan Miller, David Vagi, Robert Brazil, Kent Finne, J. Daniel Gunther, Frank Sottile, Bill Thom, Amir Modak, Emma Gonzalez, Irv Lehman, Jim Nobles, Satra Wasserman, Tara Dawn Gibson, and Marigene Riggins. My special thanks to Dr. Steven J. Greenwald, Stella Grey, and J. P. Lund for their editorial assistance. To the other friends with whom I've discussed these ideas, and who embody all variations of the political spectrum: if you don't see your name here, it's probably because I didn't want to embarrass you!

I have been greatly influenced by the writings of George Orwell, Aldous Huxely, Whittaker Chambers, Ayn Rand, Steven Barry, John Ross, James L. Pate, James Bovard, Jeff Cooper, and Gerry Spence, among others. Although not a member for personal reasons, I have found the John Birch Society to be an intelligent source of information for many of the topics discussed herein.

I stand in admiration before the thoughts and examples provided by George Washington, Thomas Jefferson, James Madison, Patrick Henry, and others of America's founders, as well as Frederick Bastiat, Friedrich Nietzsche, and Aleister Crowley.

Thanks to Frater Superior Hymenaeus Beta of Ordo Templi Orientis for permission to reprint *Liber Oz* and Crowley's letter on its relation to American liberty. Thanks also to Mr. Akram Elias of the Capital Communications Group for permission to reprint Imad Musa's translation of the Letter to the Terrorists.

Any errors of thought or fact that exist in this book are a consequence of my own lack of understanding of the problem.

Contents

FOREWORD

They who would give up essential liberty for temporary security,
deserve neither liberty or security. — Benjamin Franklin

I wonder if the brilliant Franklin could even have imagined our modern political discourse and its apparent goal of transforming society into both a nursery and a nursing home under the dual mantra of "Education and Healthcare." This collection of essays, written over the last ten years, attempts to presage the consequences of such a philosophy. Its point of view is that of an unabashed individualist who believes the freest society will bring forth the greatest good for the greatest number. If you are looking for a government plan to save your life or ease your burden, you might wish to seek elsewhere.

The book is divided in two parts. The first half is a series of my essays on Liberty and Tyranny. The second half presents the reference material for my assertions in the first.

- STEPS ALONG THE WAY discusses some of the personal transformative experiences that brought about my own passionate interest in government and political ideology.

- AN INTRODUCTION TO POLITICS is an overall look at competing political philosophies at work in the modern world. Statism and collectivism are defined and contrasted with libertarianism and individualism.

- WACO: ASK NOT FOR WHOM THE BELL TOLLS highlights the quintessential modern embodiment of America's embrace of statism. Eighty-six people died in the name of a $200 tax stamp, while the world's media endlessly parroted its government-written script.

- SEPTEMBER 11, 2001 REMEMBERED is a very topical follow up to my earlier book *The Templars and the Assassins: The Militia of Heaven*, which studied the concept of religious killing in both Islam and Christianity during the Crusades. It traces the roots and history of Islamic fundamentalism, and offers suggestions for a reasonable posture on the part of Western civilization. The Letter to the Terrorists reinforces the seriousness of my own conclusions.

- PULLING LIBERTY'S TEETH further analyzes the efforts of modern collectivists to overturn the unique freedoms on which America is based. It focuses on the campaign to strip American citizens of our unalienable right to defend life and property.

- GODDESSES, GUNS AND GUTS presents my understanding of the need to embrace transcendent values as a means of enforcing the self discipline required to function as a free person. Its title implies its universality and open ended possibilities. Atheists and agnostics may substitute the term "Moral Code."

- SUGGESTED ACTIONS offers some ideas to expand your personal freedom, communicate the importance of freedom to others, and asks some questions designed to stimulate thought beyond the confines of the modern media trance.

- LIBER OZ, a statement published by the English master Aleister Crowley during World War II, presents what I consider to be the ideal statement of the political rights of any individual courageous enough to live up to the responsibilities that freedom entails.

- The three appendices are divided between source materials of alternate political visions. I call appendix one THE LANGUAGE OF FREEDOM. It includes the most important American founding documents as well as all amendments to the U.S. Constitution. My introductory essay discusses not only the context and the uniqueness of the American experiment, but directly confronts the demoralizing issue of American slavery.

- Appendix two is called THE LANGUAGE OF TYRANNY and provides a comprehensive look at the UN's founding materials and treaties. I guarantee you will be amazed at both the sheer hubris and utter banality of what you will be reading. I have typographically highlighted or lightly annotated the most egregious examples. My introduction helps to place the founding of the UN in its historical context as part of the expansion of Soviet communism, and asks perhaps the most important political question any modern man or woman will ever confront.

- Appendix three is called THE LANGUAGE OF TREASON. It publishes a Kennedy administration policy paper presented by the president to the UN in 1962. It unambiguously exposes the goals of those who seek greater involvement with the UN. In my intro-ductory essay, I describe this document as "the smoking gun."

- Finally I include a lightly annotated list of the 50 best books I rec-ommend to any reader who cares to further his or her studies of these issues.

One issue that should be addressed at the outset is my seemingly U.S.-centric approach. This is neither jingoistic nor meant to imply disrespect to friends and readers in any other country. My studies have led me to the conclusion that the political philosophy of Amer-ica's founders was designed to create the freest and most prosperous nation the world has ever known. Unfortunately, I do not consider the modern United States to be an example of adherence to these unique roots. America's first sustained turning away from the Con-stitutional compact took place at the time of the Civil War. Less than two generations later, the establishment of the Federal Reserve, the graduated income tax, the popular election of senators, and the interventionist policies of World War I all occurred within less than a decade. The administration of Franklin Roosevelt cemented America's drift away from our founding principles.

While I pray that the U.S. will return to the philosophy of lim-ited government that is our birthright, I know of no other country in the world today that still enjoys the relative amount of freedom cel-ebrated by the average American. My fondest hope for this book is that the ideas expressed may find points of resonance within readers sufficient to encourage each to meditate on the personal value he or she places on freedom, and to act accordingly.

Steps Along the Way

Writing this book has indeed been a strange experience. In early April of 1993, my friend, Christopher Hyatt, and I agreed to do a book on secret societies. My task would be to define secret societies, then to compile a history of a number we felt were seminal to the Western Esoteric Tradition. He would provide scientific studies of psychological data he had collected over the years on members of certain modern secret societies. We would then close with an expression of our beliefs in the value, or lack thereof, of the process of secret society membership, and include suggestions to improve one's experience should one wish to join, or is already a member of, such a group.

I was confident in my ability to handle the project as I had done several years of intense research into mystical secret societies during the early to mid-80's. Some of this was published in my essay entitled "An Introduction to the History of the O.T.O." in *Equinox* Vol. III, No. 10 in 1986. I dutifully compiled a list of books and got to work. What I did not count on was the enormous psychological impact of two then-recent events that have colored my world view more than any I can remember for many years. They also became, nearly against my will, such prominent influences in my life that the one book became two, both quite different than intended. As my experience during the first of these events was seminal, a retelling is in order.

In late August 1992 I became ill and ran a high fever. A dear friend was getting married that weekend; I had to miss the wedding, was confined to bed and generally miserable. I saw a small article in that sacred scroll of "All the News Fit to Print," *The New York Times*. It concerned a "standoff" at Ruby Ridge, Idaho, between approximately 300 government agents, armed with every weapon Uncle Sam could muster short of nuclear missiles, and a "kook" named Randy Weaver. His 14-year-old son had been shot in the back by Federal agents, and his wife had been killed by an FBI sniper. Randy Weaver himself was wounded and holed up in his mountain cabin with another friend also wounded by Federal agents, his two older daughters, and a baby. *The Times* printed a photo of some government agents with the letters ATF hugely displayed on one agent's back. I at once realized such large letters were designed to lessen the chances of killing one of their own *when shooting American citizens in the back.* I searched the few paragraphs of the article over and over for a clue to Randy Weaver's crime, and could only find vague suggestions of "weapons violations." Weaver was described as a neo-Nazi racist, and that was basically that.

As a Jew, with one child of mixed race, neo-Nazi racists are not exactly my cup of tea, nor do I suspect I'm their's. But there I was with this incredibly high fever. And I lay my head down and closed my eyes — and my soul literally entered Randy Weaver's cabin, and my psyche became conjoined with his for a time. And I experienced his torture. I felt his grief, his terror, his horror, through every fiber of my being. And I came out of it and cried, and I told my wife how sad he was, and what a horrible thing it was to have your son and your wife killed, and all those murderers outside your cabin with their guns, and the signs on their backs so they won't hurt each other when they shoot your children in the back. And to be painted by the press as some subhuman scum whom it was the government's duty to exterminate.

The world seemed very different when that fever broke. The country of my birth especially seemed different.

I immersed myself in an attempt to understand what had happened. I had a fair degree of exposure to political conspiracies during my earlier research into mystical secret societies. Yet I had largely bypassed the sinister forces of conspiracy in favor of the Lightbearers whose wisdom I sought. The experience with Weaver forced me to search the other side. After months of sleepless nights and many thousands of pages of reading, I was on the verge of a nervous breakdown. I knew I had to stop, and finally I began to pull myself out of it sometime between mid January and early February of 1993. Guess what happened next? The actual facts concerning the federal assault on the Branch Davidian church are still so little known, a decade later, and so important, that I am including a separate chapter here on the Waco holocaust.

People are often startled when this studious looking, graying refugee from the 1960s espouses a political philosophy that, to some, seems more akin to Attila the Hun than either Jimmy Carter or Tom Hayden. How could someone who has taken so much LSD not cheerfully support the one-world, internationalist, corporate-socialist, UN directed global village?

Here is the reason. Liberty has been the entire basis of my life quest. I have used every technique I could find to maximize my

Liberty: meditation, ritual magick, sex, drugs, sobriety, philosophy, personal economics, and career choice. I have come to believe that political liberty is an essential component of spiritual liberty.

I too embraced socialism as a youth. My heart was torn by injustice. Racism, poverty, hunger, war, pestilence — all seemed curable if only we could muster the will to unite and stop them. How else could this be accomplished other than through the concerted efforts of a centrally planned system whose over-reaching power could proceed unobstructed to these lofty goals? A letter to my parents in the summer of 1966 confirms that I was aware this would involve compulsion. However, at age eighteen I believed the greater good outweighed the rights of the individual — a belief I no longer hold.

A series of warnings about socialism came in the fall of 1966, when I served as a volunteer political activist in Washington, D.C. through the work/study program at my college. I worked for several months as a research assistant to the last white lawyer representing SNCC, the Student Non-Violent Coordinating Committee. (Stokely Carmichael had proclaimed Black Power that spring.) I met many of the big names in the civil rights and anti-war movement. I noticed that a number of them seemed either mean-spirited or unhappy with their lives. I detected their cravings for power. I realized my political work would merely help substitute one group of power-mad neurotics for another — and either accomplish nothing or make the situation worse. The end for me came when I had a rare, relaxed, private conversation with my boss. I asked him if he thought our work might actually be helping the communists, as many people then claimed. He told me that he frankly didn't care, and that he did not reject communism outright. I did, and left soon thereafter. Only later did I understand that socialism is the first step on the road to communism.

I became aware of the spirit, and turned inward. In a "position statement" to myself at the end of 1966, I defined meditation and the spiritual life as the sole means of achieving the humanitarian goals I sought. I believed then, and still do, that the salvation of humanity needs to be achieved one person, one mind, one soul at a time. That only by rooting out the evil and ignorance within oneself is it truly possible to root out evil and ignorance in the world. I sought, and continue to seek, spiritual enlightenment.

In mid-1967, I met a new college roommate who became a close friend. A member of the cutting-edge communist Progressive Labor Party, he once explained that, despite our friendship, when the revolution came I would be one of those rounded up and executed. My bourgeois beliefs in the sanctity of the individual were counter-productive to the "will of the people." I now understood what I was up against. (After spending many miserable years trying to organize factory workers, this person continues to spread his communist philosophy as a tenured college professor.)

A decade later, I had begun to work as a freelance book designer. A client asked me to give her my price for doing a project. But she warned me that a non-profit, government-funded book production studio was also quoting on the job. I mentioned this to my mentor in dismay, and he laughed. He suggested I ask my client how she would like the Post Office to produce her book! When I think of the socialist goal of a world bureaucracy run by "experts" and civil servants, I ask myself: How would I like the Post Office to run the world?

I also reject the collectivist police state because of my family background. I will never abandon the childhood pride inspired by my father's tale of his father's arrival in America, among the early twentieth century wave of immigrants. My grandfather was a 16-year-old peasant boy during the Cossack pogroms conducted against Jews by the Russian government. A drunken soldier locked him and a group of villagers in a barn and began to set fire to it. My grandfather shoved a pitchfork through the barn door and killed the soldier, saving many lives. Needless to say he was forced to flee. Perhaps this bit of family history, combined with my knowledge of the murder of many relatives on my mother's side by the Nazis, leaves me with a tendency to be less than trustful of government in general.

Spiritually, I embrace the teachings of Aleister Crowley and *The Book of the Law*.[1] A natural corollary of this is that I believe in Divine Inspiration. I also believe that *The Book of the Law* was neither the first nor the last time divine inspiration penetrated human consciousness. I believe the American Constitution and its Bill of Rights to be an inspired model of the type of society later articulated by Crowley in *Liber Oz* (a short tract written in 1941, that expressed the political philosophy of *The Book of the Law* in words of

---

[1] I should make clear at the outset that the opinions expressed in this book are my own. They are not intended to be either an analysis of Crowley's political thought, nor representative of any policies, doctrines, or beliefs of the mystical society he led Ordo Templi Orientis (O.T.O.). I would expect some members of the O.T.O. to disagree strongly with a number of the ideas expressed in these pages.

one syllable). What makes the ideas of both *Liber Oz* and the Bill of Rights so radical is their guarantee of nearly unlimited personal liberty and individual rights. If these two documents are examples of secret societies engineering social change — Brethren, let us pray! Both are included in this book.

Implicit in seeking to maximize individual liberty is a recognition of the divinity inherent within human beings ("endowed by their Creator"). Quoting *The Book of the Law*, "Every man and every woman is a star," and "thou hast no right but to do thy will." In my opinion, these statements posit both a will to do, and an attainable celestial nature at the root of the self. The reigning political goal of a society built on these principles must be the encouragement of maximum individual liberty for the most unfettered growth of the inner potential.

I watch with sorrow as American society willingly embraces the socialist doctrine of the corporate/welfare state, like so many sheep herding themselves into the pen to be shorn. I am reminded of Crowley's remarks about religion. If the reader will simply substitute "the State" for "God" in the following extract, I think the point will have been made.

> The type of tailless simian who finds himself a mere forked radish in a universe of giants clamouring for *hors d'oeuvres* must take refuge from Reality in Freudian phantasies of "God." He winces at the touch of Truth; and shivers at his nakedness in Nature. He therefore invents a cult of fear and shame, and makes it presumption and blasphemy to possess courage and self-respect.[2]

In mid-May of 2001, the first volume of this series was published. *The Templars and Assassins: The Militia of Heaven* provides an in-depth description of the two mystical secret societies who have most influenced today's spiritual and magical practices. In the present volume, you will read about the political and cultural conspiracies whose object is the enslavement of America in preparation for a global tyranny that fulfills ambitions dating back to at least ancient Egypt. It is my fervent hope that the knowledge imparted here will

[2] *The Law Is For All*, Aleister Crowley, ed. Louis Wilkinson and Hymenaeus Beta, New Falcon Publications, Tempe, AZ, 1996, p. 152.

encourage readers to continue to investigate these ideas for themselves and enlist in the fight against the possibility of that dark future.

The content of this book will reveal my slant toward Second Amendment concerns. Among my peers, most are concerned with First Amendment advocacy. Fourth Amendment issues similarly motivate my friends. However the linchpin of all the freedoms we enjoy, Liberty's Teeth, is the Second Amendment. Therefore I make no apologies for bringing this subject to your attention.

Finally, I believe each human being has an inborn spiritual destiny which it is his or her task to learn and fulfill. "Do what thou wilt shall be the whole of the Law."[3] I believe that many people who are "into the occult" (or for that matter, almost any other form of spiritual pursuit) have been guilty of burying their heads in the sand — prancing around candlelit rooms, or sitting in meditation, imagining themselves as conscious beings growing in enlightenment. Enlightenment is based on Freedom. Without a determination to extend that freedom to all beings and becomings, we are nothing but mindless acolytes of the very forces of Darkness against whom we draw our Circles. Meditate on this the next time you watch a TV news report, for thus is the arch-demon described in *The Vision and the Voice*:

> Choronzon hath no form, because he is the maker of all form; and so rapidly he changeth from one to the other as he may best think fit to seduce those whom he hateth, the servants of the Most High.
>
> Thus taketh he the form of a beautiful woman, or of a wise and holy man, or of a serpent that writheth upon the earth ready to sting.[4]

---

[3] Crowley called Do what thou wilt "the most sublimely austere ethical code ever uttered, despite its apparent license ..." *Magick In Theory and Practice*, Lecram Press, Paris, 1929, reprinted Magickal Childe Publishing, Inc., NY, 1990, p. 262.
[4] *The Vision and The Voice With Commentary*, *Equinox Vol. IV, No. 2.*, Aleister Crowley, et al., Samuel Weiser, Inc., York Beach, 1998, p. 165.

An Introduction
to Politics

*If you want a picture of the future, imagine a boot stamping on
a human face forever.* — George Orwell, *1984*

I take full responsibility. The buck stops here.
— Janet Reno on the deaths of the Branch Davidians

The U.S. Constitutional Model of Freedom

The American Bill of Rights represents the first time in history
that individual sovereignty was legally codified as *primary*, and
government sovereignty as *secondary*. The Declaration of Independence spells out America's founders' understanding of the origin of
our rights in no uncertain terms, "We hold these Truths to be self-
evident, that all Men are ... endowed by their Creator with certain
unalienable Rights ... " These words indicate an inherent respect for
human nature that, I believe, is an absolute prerequisite for a vision
of human freedom.

The inviolate supremacy of the "unalienable rights" acknowledged in the Bill of Rights is protected, in the American system, *from*
the State. The "human rights" acknowledged by the UN and other
World Government models are conditional upon the will *of* the
State. They are contingent rights, more accurately *privileges*, given or
dispensed by the State. One cannot over-emphasize the importance
of the difference between these two points of view. Quite simply, it
is the difference between freedom and tyranny.

The appendix provides incontrovertible proof of these assertions. I have included full texts of the American Declaration of Independence, the U.S. Constitution, the Bill of Rights, and later
Amendments. These are juxtaposed with material from the primary
UN declarations and covenants. The UN documents will demon-
strate that every "right" promised by the UN can be taken away at
the will of the government, as soon as the cause of "public order" is
invoked. Nowhere in the UN scheme is there any individual right of
self defense. Perfectly embodying the police state or military

dictatorship, the only armed people in the UN's vision are police, selected bureaucrats, and soldiers.

By contrast, the U.S. Constitution purposely set up an inefficient government. Thomas Jefferson spoke of an America government, "shackled by the chains of the Constitution." Our system of checks and balances was designed to create a continual state of tension in which the power drives of one branch of government would be offset by those of another. The Legislative, Executive, and Judicial branches of the federal government compete among themselves. The popular House of Representatives is pitted against the patrician Senate. The national government is ideally contending with a group of tenacious state governments. Local and county governments contend with each other. All governmental power groups are balanced against the most important group of all, a free and self-determined citizenry by whose will and consent these various government units are formed and empowered. The people themselves are checked against their predictable excesses by a written code of law, the Constitution, which both enumerates rights held by the people and defines the legitimate activities of government. The founders were well aware of the dangers of democracy — whose anti-symbol is the lynch mob, the apotheosis of unrestrained majority rule. America is designed to be a representative democratic Republic.[1]

THE "NEW WORLD ORDER" AS A MODEL OF POLITICAL CONTROL

America's heritage of individual sovereignty is under sustained attack by proponents of a *New World Order*, whose cradle-to-grave security-and-obedience paradigm is inimical to the founding principles of this country. Americans are daily barraged by an endless media parade of those who camouflage their lust for power and control under the banners of Compassion, Democracy, Global Interdependence, and Resource Management. We face a relentless assault designed to persuade us to sacrifice our precious liberty in the name of Collective Security — to welcome an enforced subservience of the individual to the "common good."

Before proceeding further, it is essential to examine the meaning

---

[1] A simple democracy is best illustrated by the example of two wolves and a sheep voting on what to have for lunch. In a republic, the sheep would be armed.

of "government." Reduced to its most basic essence, the nature of government is force. From the ability to enforce compliance with traffic lights and speed limits, to collect taxes, to enforce laws against thievery and murder, to wage war with vast armies and terrible weapons, government is force. By its very definition therefore, government is always a potential threat to those who fall within its sphere of influence. America's founders recognized this simple truism and sought to protect themselves and their progeny by severely limiting government. Proponents of the "Global Village" model appear far less concerned with the dangers of abuse of power.

Those who suggest unfettered government as the means to insure collective security would receive little validation from the statistics presented by Professor R. J. Rummel.[2] In all the international and civil wars of the twentieth century from 1900–1987, Rummel estimates that at least thirty-eight million soldiers and civilians died. In the same period, he estimates that a minimum of one hundred seventy million people were starved, gassed and otherwise slaughtered by their governments during times of peace. Thus in the first eighty-seven years of the twentieth century, a person was four times more likely to have been murdered by his government during peacetime than killed by his country's enemies during war. The Soviet Union was responsible for some sixty-two million civilian deaths. Communist China, gracious host of the United Nations Conference on the Rights of Women and proxy owner of the Panama Canal, was responsible for an estimated thirty-six million murders. Germany's National Socialists killed an estimated twenty-one million civilians.

When America rejected the League of Nations in 1918, those who had offered the treaty decided upon a long range plan to educate the American people into an acceptance of world government. After some eighty years, an increasingly large percentage of self-professed rational people feel that a form of world government is inevitable. Check the lower part of your TV screen the next time you see a "talking head." Chances are, he or she will be identified as a member of the Council on Foreign Relations (CFR), formed in 1921 to encourage Americans to support international law.

Don't forget that the consequence of accepting international law is the abandonment of American law. International treaties

---

[2] R. J. Rummel, *Death by Government*, Transaction Publishers, New Brunswick, 1994, pp. 3–4.

supercede U.S. law, as is spelled out in Article 6, Paragraph 2 of the Constitution (see page 134). The increasing frequency of global accords should therefore give pause to all. To the dismay of many, the U.S. Supreme Court has increasingly been citing agreements among European states in its justifications for its rulings on questions of U.S. law. Despite his solemn oath to uphold the U.S. Constitution, Justice Stephen Breyer stated in July of 2003 that the Constitution may well be unsuited for the age of globalization.[3]

During the Kennedy administration, a State Department document entitled *Freedom from War*[4] methodically laid out a blueprint for the surrender of American sovereignty to a United Nations led world government. This plan was personally presented to the United Nations by President Kennedy on September 25, 1961. It is still the official policy of the U.S. Government. Some particularly telling points enunciated therein include the following:

> This new program provides for the progressive reduction of the war-making capabilities of nations and the simultaneous strengthening of international institutions to settle disputes and maintain the peace.

> There is an inseparable relationship between the scaling down of national armaments on the one hand and the building up of international peace-keeping machinery and institutions on the other.

> The over-all goal of the United States is a free, secure, and peaceful world ... in which adjustment to change takes place in accordance with the principles of the United Nations.

> In Stage III progressive controlled disarmament and continuously developing principles and procedures of international law would proceed to a point *where no state would have the military power to challenge the progressively strengthened UN Peace Force* and all international disputes would be settled according to the agreed principles of international conduct. [Emphasis mine]

---

[3] *The New American Magazine*, July 28, 2003, "Reigning Supreme" by William Norman Grigg.
[4] *Freedom From War, The United States Program for General and Complete Disarmament in a Peaceful World*, Department of State Publication 7277, September 1961.

While these statements may reasonably be construed as treason, at the very least, they make clear that in order for the Globalist political agenda to succeed, America must surrender its independence as a nation. The enormous ramifications of this course of action are rarely mentioned. One advocate of world government explained the lack of candor when he suggested that, "... an end run around national sovereignty, eroding it piece by piece, will accomplish much more than the old-fashioned frontal assault."[5] *Freedom From War* is published in its entirety in appendix 3.

Building The Nanny State

No one today is unconcerned about the critical issues facing our modern world. Indeed, the complexity of the conditions encountered by 21st century humanity might well be viewed as an invigorating challenge to strong-minded, optimistic, and creative people. Instead, a depressed and impotent spirit pervades much of our nation. Widespread cynicism has been erected upon the collapse of morality. America has abandoned her vision of the sovereignty and competence of the individual, as well as her acceptance of a transcendental reality against which our decisions are to be weighed.

The leaders of the Collectivist movement are people in government, finance, education, and the media who feel they are better qualified to run our lives than we are. A particularly telling example of this observation is the following statement by then First Lady Hillary Clinton to Dennis Hastert, at the time the Illinois Congressman who chaired the Republican task force on health care. Hastert described a June 1993 meeting with Mrs. Clinton, part of an effort to craft a bipartisan approach to health care, in which she expressed her rejection of medical savings accounts in these words:

> We can't do that. The first reason is with the medical savings account, people have to act on their own and make their own decisions about health care. And they have to make sure that they get the inoculations and the preventative care that they need, and

[5] Richard N. Gardner, "The Hard Road to World Order," *Foreign Affairs*, April 1974, quoted by James Perloff in *Shadows of Power*, Western Islands Publishers, Appleton, 1988, pp. 11–12.

we just think that people will skip too much because in a medical savings account if you don't spend it, you get to keep it.... We just think people will be too focused on saving money and they won't get the care for their children and themselves that they need. We think the government, by saying "you have to make this schedule. You have to have your kids in for inoculations here, you have to do a prescreening here, you have to do this" — the government will make better decisions than the people will make, and people will be healthier because of it.... We can't trust the American people to make those type of choices. [T]he second reason is, with a medical savings account, savings are [like] an IRA ... We can't afford to have that money go to the private sector. The money has to go to the federal government because the federal government will spend that money better than the private sector will spend it."[6]

We are sacrificing our liberty to these busybodies because they seem to *value* it more than we do. The absurdity of the lengths and intrusiveness to which they are prepared to go was demonstrated in 1993 when they pounced into our very beds at Antioch College with the school's widely publicized sexual speech code. Indeed, the "politically correct" phenomena of the 1990s might be humorous if its implications were not so alarming. Soon these personality types will demand we make them responsible for giving us permission to produce children. Later they will insist on determining our children's schooling, profession, and place of residence (all in the name of global ecology, crime-prevention, human rights, etc., *ad nauseam*).

The price of freedom is eternal vigilance. And we have been asleep at the wheel. The American people's very ability to think, debate, and rationally examine ideas is being worn down by an educational system the purpose of which is to produce empty-headed sensualists, whose materialistic concerns keep them in a perpetual state of tractability. Decades before the psychic nourishment of "Generation X" by MTV, *et al*, one of the philosophers of freedom, Ayn Rand, wrote the following prophetic words of warning.

In any given period of history, a culture is to be judged by its dominant philosophy, by the prevalent trends of its intellectual life as

---

[6] David Brock, *The Seduction of Hillary Clinton*, NY: Free Press, 1996, pp. 333–4.

expressed in morality, in politics, in economics, in art.... What are the intellectual values or resources offered by the present guardians of our culture? In philosophy, we are taught that man's mind is impotent, that reality is unknowable, that knowledge is an illusion, and reason a superstition. In psychology, we are told that man is a helpless automaton, determined by forces beyond his control, motivated by innate depravity. In literature, we are shown a line-up of murderers, dipsomaniacs, drug addicts, neurotics and psychotics as representatives of man's soul — and are invited to identify our own among them — with the belligerent assertions that life is a sewer, a foxhole or a rat race, with the whining injunctions that we must love everything, except virtue, and forgive everything, except greatness.[7]

The Age of the Expert

Those who embrace the collectivist ideal have rejected a basic philosophical assumption about humanity that underlies all dreams of Freedom: that within our species is a potential for harmonious development when each does the bidding of his true nature to the fullest. No less an authority than Carroll Quigley, author of *Tragedy and Hope*, has declared this a "superstition," an example of nineteenth century romanticism. Former President Clinton fondly acknowledged Quigley as his mentor during his 1992 Inauguration speech. Quigley well describes certain key aspects of what might be called the vision of an *inherently successful* humanity in the following words.

[L]iberalism was based on an almost universally accepted nineteenth-century superstition known as the "community of interests." This strange, and unexamined, belief held that there really existed, in the long run, a community of interests between the members of a society ... a possible social pattern in which each member of society would be secure, free, and prosperous, and that this pattern could be achieved by a process of adjustment so that each person could fall into that place in the pattern to which his innate abilities entitled him. This implied two corollaries which the nineteenth century was prepared to accept: (1) that human

[7] Ayn Rand, *For the New Intellectual*, NY: Signet, 1961, pp. 10–11.

abilities are innate and can only be distorted or suppressed by social discipline and (2) *that each individual is the best judge of his own self-interest*. All these together form the doctrine of the "community of interests," a doctrine which maintained that if each individual does what seems best for himself, the result, in the long run, will be best for society as a whole. [emphasis mine][8]

Lest that cause us any anxiety, some 800 pages later, Quigley makes it clear that this vision has been deemed inoperative. He explains that twentieth century realism has finally come to terms with man's intrinsically flawed nature. Social scientists have identified humanity as *inherently unsuccessful*. We have entered the Age of the Expert. Social planners are heralded as the new deities who will bring order out of the chaos of mankind's unbridled and destructive passions. They will channel our base natures into constructive byways. Quigley writes,

> [I]t is increasingly clear that, in the twentieth century, the expert will replace the industrial tycoon in control of the economic system even as he will replace the democratic voter in control of the political system. This is because planning will inevitably replace *laissez faire* in the relationship between the two systems. This planning may not be single or unified, but it will be *planning*, in which the main framework and operational forces of the system will be established and limited by the experts on the government side; then the experts within the big units on the economic side will do their planning within these established limitations. Hopefully, the elements of choice and freedom may survive for the ordinary individual ... But, in general, his freedom and choice will be controlled within very narrow alternatives by the fact that he will be numbered from birth and followed, as a number, through his educational training, his required military or other public service, his tax contributions, his health and medical requirements, and his final retirement and death benefits. [emphasis in original][9]

---

[8] Carroll Quigley, *Tragedy and Hope*, Angriff Press, Los Angeles, 1974, pp. 25–26.
[9] Ibid, p. 866.

Tragic Modern Warnings

The seriousness of the danger we face as a society was conclusively demonstrated at Ruby Ridge and Waco. The hooded black figures with automatic weapons are not necessarily terrorists these days — they may be federal police. After the terrible fire at Waco on April 19, 1993, our globally-compassionate political leaders strutted and fretted their hour upon the stage — each one declaring him or herself so willing to "take responsibility" for the multiple deaths that you had to wonder when their jail terms would begin. The American Civil Liberties Union (ACLU), Amnesty International, and the host of other professional conscience-mongers were so silent regarding government abuse of power against the Branch Davidian church in Waco, you could hear a dead child's whimper.

The Weaver family in Idaho was targeted by the Bureau of Alcohol, Tobacco, and Firearms (ATF) for a "sting operation." Randy Weaver was entrapped into committing a $200 federal tax violation. Desperate for funds to feed his family, Weaver agreed to shorten two used shotguns to the length demanded by an undercover ATF informant, who promised to pay cash for the weapons. Weaver shortened the barrels to within *one-third of an inch* of the legal, tax-free limit. The end result of this nonsense was that on August 21, 1992, the Weaver property was invaded by masked U.S. Marshals in ninja suits — armed with pistols, sub-machine guns, and automatic rifles — who later claimed to have just been conducting surveillance. The Marshals first shot and killed the family dog, then shot 14-year-old Sammy Weaver in the back as he ran to join his father, killing the boy instantly. One of the Marshals was shot and killed. Next, 300 federal police surrounded the Weavers' ramshackle plywood cabin, described in the media as a "fortress." An FBI sniper fired a .30 caliber bullet into Vicki Weaver's head, killing her as she cradled her ten-month-old baby in her arms. After 11 days, a severely wounded Randy Weaver surrendered. He was later acquitted of murder charges by a jury of his peers and soon set free.

The Weaver saga finally received some acknowledgment, including a reasonably fair TV movie in 1996, despite the earlier unanimous media blitz against the Weaver's "white-supremacist, armed-extremist" profile. A secret Justice Department report leaked in December 1994 acknowledged that Mrs. Weaver's Constitutional Rights were violated by the FBI's unique "rules of engagement" for that operation. The rules (instructing agents to shoot to kill any adult on sight) had been written by Richard Rogers, one of the FBI commanders who would be responsible for the deaths of the Branch Davidians eight months later. While all the money or legal precedents in the world can't bring back a son or a wife, Randy Weaver received a $3.1 million settlement from the government, although with no admission of wrongdoing on the government's part. While America's taxpayers were presented with the opportunity to cover our leaders' financial liabilities, the U.S. Marshals Service presented its highest award for valor to the jack-booted thugs who conducted the initial raid and shot young Sammy Weaver in the back. The March 1, 1996 citation praised "… their exceptional courage, their sound judgment in the face of attack, and their high degree of professional competence during the incident."[10]

Another example of the ruthless manipulation of information, and disregard for the lives of American citizens took place in the aftermath of the Oklahoma City bombing. Among many disturbing issues, the most blatant was the destruction of the crime scene. Like a replay of Waco, all forensic evidence was simply bulldozed into oblivion, leaving a litany of unanswered questions. Chief among these is the ability of an ammonium-nitrate fuel-oil bomb — exploded in an outdoor parking lot — to cause so much damage to the structure and to produce the blast pattern that resulted. Explosive experts presented eloquent scientific arguments that additional explosives must have been placed within the building. Seismographic readings in two separate locations offered independent indications of dual explosions. The physical evidence of an intact crime scene certainly could have laid these questions to rest. The devastating possibility that illegal storage of explosives by the ATF (in the same building as a children's day care center) may have caused the second explosion and collateral damage might also have been satisfactorily answered by a competent forensic investigation.

The carefully managed disclaimer of the existence of "John Doe No. 2," after one of the most widely publicized manhunts in history, is provocative, when weighed against the testimony of the many eyewitnesses who claim to have seen such an individual. The initial descriptions of McVeigh's accomplice as "looking like an Arab" are troubling. A lawsuit filed by family members of OKC victims in

[10] Robert K. Brown, in an editorial quoting from the citation, *Soldier of Fortune Magazine*, June 1996.

2002, claims that during his several visits to the Philippines, Terry Nichols (McVeigh's convicted accomplice in the bombing) was in contact with Ramzi Youssef (mastermind of the first World Trade Center bombing in 1993), and other members of the Abu Sayyaf terror group. Finally, the dark weight of prior knowledge of the bombing by federal police, through a paid government informant named Carol Howe, is too strong to ignore.[11]

The fourth example is perhaps the most troubling, if the least dramatic. World War II was the last time this country engaged in a military action that was legal under our system of government. While Roosevelt may have had indications of the attack on Pearl Harbor,[12] at least that war was fought with a formal declaration of war by Congress as required under Article I, Section 8 of the Constitution. Beginning with President Truman's UN "police-action" in Korea in 1952, to the "enforcement of UN Resolution 1441" by President Bush in Iraq in 2003, every major military campaign in the last half century has been illegal and unconstitutional. Not even the attack on the Pentagon and the World Trade Center could motivate an aetiolated Congress to exercise its Constitutional duty of declaring war on al-Qaeda and the Taliban, as it did against the Barbary pirates in 1815. Allowing the military to serve at the beck and call of a U.S. president, as has been the norm since my birth, may yield unimaginably evil consequences. Our leaders appear to consider their oaths to preserve and defend the Constitution as meaningless.

"DRUGS AND GUNS"

Even before the "fall" of the Soviet Union and the "liberation" of South Africa, the United States boasted the largest percentage of its citizens in prison in the entire world. We still hold the record.[13] In

[11] See *The New American* various issues in 1995 including May 15, June 12, August 7, and December 11. See in 1996, issues dated April 1, May 13, June 24. Issues in 1997 include February 17. See also *Final Report on the Bombing of the Alfred P. Murrah Federal Building*, Oklahoma City, The Oklahoma Bombing Investigation Committee, 2001. Attorney Stephan Jones interview posted 10/22/02, available at FreeRepublic.com http://209.157.64.200/focus/news/773917/posts#comment.
[12] See among others Robert B. Sinnett, *Day of Deceipt: The Truth About FDR and Pearl Harbor*, NY, Free Press, 2001.
[13] *Christian Science Monitor*, August 18, 2003, "US Notches World's Highest Incarceration Rate." One in 37 adults have spent time in prison. The Justice Department

1990, 50% of new inmates in New York were imprisoned solely for the sale or possession of drugs. We apparently need more prisons to make room for criminals as well as pot smokers. By what authority is the Government empowered to imprison people who are not committing crimes *against others?* The First Amendment guarantees free expression; the Fourth Amendment guarantees privacy; the Ninth and Tenth Amendments tell the Federal Government exactly where it must stop in enacting legislation. If a person commits a crime while under the influence of drugs, he should certainly be imprisoned. If a person commits a crime with a gun, that person should also be punished. But the operative phrase is "If a person commits a crime," not "drugs," or "guns."

The Clinton administration worked overtime to craft legislation and rally public support to subvert the Fourth Amendment by authorizing warrantless searches in public housing and on our nation's roadways to combat "drugs and guns." Laws regarding vehicular searches became increasingly freed from the restraint of Constitutionally mandated search warrants in the decades since the asset seizure frenzy began in 1970 with the so-called War on Drugs. James Bovard writes, "... federal agents can now seize private property under 200 different statutes. From 1985 to 1991, the number of federal seizures of property under asset forfeiture laws increased by 1,500 percent."[14] Bovard also succinctly states that, "Private property marks the boundary between the citizen and the State. The degree of respect the State shows for property rights will largely determine how much privacy, autonomy, and independence the citizen has."[15]

The September 11, 2001 al-Qaeda attacks on America were a dream come true for the statists. All the carefully crafted regulations that had been simmering in the totalitarian pot for over a decade were served up by Congress in the ironically named "Patriot Act." Search warrants will become a quaint relic of the past if this monstrous legislation is allowed to survive. Yet those who squawk loudest about Attorney General John Ashcroft's supposed disregard for civil liberties must have a very short attention span. Every aspect of the

---

estimates that the chances of serving time during one's life are 1 in 3 for Black males, 1 in 6 for Hispanic males, and 1 in 17 for White males.

[14] *Lost Rights, The Destruction of American Liberty*, James Bovard, , St. Martin' Griffin, NY, 1995, p. 11.

[15] *Ibid.*, p. 10.

"Patriot Act" was fully drafted (and most had already been rejected by Congress) in the decade before the bin Laden attack.

President Bush, who was elected in no small part because of the support of the National Rifle Association (NRA) in certain key states, has pledged to sign the reauthorization of Clinton's disastrous, inane, and unconstitutional "assault weapons" ban.[16] At the very moment when American citizens have been specifically and publicly targeted for death by foreign and domestic enemies with a track record of successful attacks, "our" government responds by attempting to further inhibit our capacity to defend ourselves. Who are these people? Why do we continue to pay their salaries?

PERSONAL RESPONSIBILITY

Modern America has developed a confusion between parental and government authority. We have also become unwilling to face two inevitable facts of life. The first is *risk*. The second is *pain*. The psychiatrist first replaced the priest, and was himself replaced by prozac. Avoidance of pain is a natural and necessary survival reaction for a species. However, traditional American values — in which the

[16] Words have meaning. An assault rifle is a military firearm that is capable of both semi-automatic firing (one bullet is launched each time the trigger is pulled), or fully automatic firing (numerous bullets are launched as the trigger is held back until either it is released or the ammunition exhausted). The (unconstitutional) National Firearms Act of 1934, amended in 1986, heavily regulates automatic weapons or "assault weapons." The 1994 falsely titled Assault Weapons Ban regulates rifles that *look like* assault rifles. It should be more properly titled "Assault Rifle Look-Alike Ban" or "Semi-Automatic Scary-Looking Rifle Ban." Semi-automatic rifles have been in civilian hands for over a hundred years. Most people cannot visually tell the difference between an assault rifle and a semi-automatic military style rifle. This confusion was used by the gun prohibition forces to ram through the 1994 law. When the ban was passed, less than one percent of all gun crimes were committed by people using these semi-automatic military style rifles. Thus, as predicted, the ban has had no effect on crime . What it has done, is inconvenience millions of Americans, dramatically raised the price of legal firearms, and often lowered the quality of the necessary accessories for these weapons. It has also criminalized non-violent behavior, led to gun confiscation of legally owned property in numerous states including California and New York, and provided the opportunity for all kinds of misinformation to be fed to the American population by politicians, gun prohibitionists, and the press. For more information on this important subject, please visit http://www.awbansun-set.com.

virtues of courage, persistence, and self-reliance are emphasized — have been progressively eroded in modern culture. The reason is simple. It is easier to control sheep than goats. The method is ingenious. While it has taken many decades to effectively organize, it is quite easy to understand. An alliance between government, the news media, and the state-mandated foundation-funded educational system has been progressively indoctrinating the population for nearly a hundred years.

At the same time that we acknowledge a persistent campaign against the American citizen, we assert that personal individual evasion of moral responsibility is the key to the slavery we are substituting daily for the freedom that is the birthright and responsibility of every citizen of this nation. A citizenry gets the government it deserves. We must work with diligence to strengthen ourselves as individuals to preserve our national heritage. The keys are self-discipline and education. An informed electorate — schooled in the foundations of American political thought, and conscious of the machinations of those seeking to undermine it — can be trusted to elect and guide its politicians. Each of us who escapes the brainwashing is another mind (and vote) free to demand the conservation of our Liberty.

While today's society is vastly different than that of 1776, two things have not changed at all. One is human nature. The other is human potential. The Declaration of Independence, the Constitution, and the Bill of Rights are the most profound and liberating political blueprints ever developed by the mind of man. Each one takes careful heed of human nature while celebrating human potential. In contrast, the pathetic, loser-by-definition, guilt-ridden, handwringing and cringing of the New World Order crowd are merely sophisticated psychological tactics designed to induce subservience.

I accept the concept of our nation's moral responsibility to humanity. I am also aware that not one starving belly or empty wallet can be effectively filled by forcibly emptying the belly or wallet of another. True compassion and true idealism demand we honor and defend the uniquely American philosophical underpinnings of individual sovereignty. America can share this precious vision of Liberty with all the world — by example. Our strength and joy can serve as a worldwide beacon of hope and light.

WACO

ASK NOT FOR WHOM THE BELL TOLLS

*Although we give lip service to the notion of freedom, we know
the government is no longer the servant of the people but, at last,
has become the people's master. We have stood by like timid
sheep while the wolf killed — first the weak, then the strays, then
those on the outer edge of the flock, until at last the entire flock
belonged to the wolf.*
— Gerry Spence, *From Freedom to Slavery*

On February 28, 1993 nearly 100 heavily armed federal police
descended upon a religious group outside Waco, Texas. A fierce
gun battle resulted. Six sect members were killed along with four
ATF agents. On April 19, after a 51 day standoff, the church was
burned to the ground in a raging inferno that took the lives of 74
people, plus two unborn children.

THE BRANCH DAVIDIAN CHURCH. This obscure sect, a reform movement of the Seventh Day Adventists, was founded by a Bulgarian
immigrant named Victor Houteff. He began his preaching in Los
Angeles in 1929. Houteff and his followers eventually moved to
Texas and established themselves outside Waco at the first Mt.
Carmel Center in 1934. In 1957, they moved to the 77-acre ranch
forever etched in the American psyche. The group was mostly self-
sufficient — raising much of their own food, making their own
clothes, and living communally. Some residents had jobs in the area,
and, in recent years, they had established a custom auto restoration
and repair business in town.

David Koresh had been the leader of the group since 1987. He
was 33 years old when he died, an accomplished biblical student, as
well as an enigmatic and troubling personality. He held unorthodox
views of sexuality— strangely similar to the 12th century Cathars.
He was an ardent firearms enthusiast and collector, a rock musician,
custom car devotee, and the father of a number of children by several different wives, most of whom lived together with him at Mt.
Carmel. His congregation included approximately 130 people.

THE BUREAU OF ALCOHOL, TOBACCO AND FIREARMS. The ATF was founded in 1791 by Treasury Secretary Alexander Hamilton to enforce a federal whiskey tax. They reached their proud apogee during Prohibition when the Untouchable Elliot Ness fought Al Capone in the streets of Chicago. When Prohibition was nullified in 1933, the agency's prospects were uncertain until passage of the unconstitutional National Firearms Act of 1934.

The February 28th Waco assault was an attempt to gain favorable publicity prior to the annual Congressional appropriations hearing scheduled for March 10. The agency had been under fire. A series of abusive raids against peaceable gun owners during the late 80s and early 90s were coming under increased scrutiny. On January 12, 60 Minutes broadcast allegations of sexual harassment of ATF female agents — and reports of intimidation and punishment of victims and witnesses who had pressed their claims. Charges of racial discrimination had also been filed against the bureau by a group of black agents in October of 1992. Leaders hoped the raid would be a public relations victory that would set it all right with the new, anti-gun Clinton administration. Dramatic television footage of a commando-style action would also intimidate both religious cultists and gun owners.

The agency never intended to arrest Koresh peacefully, despite the fact that their search and arrest warrants required them do so. ATF had practiced the raid for months at Ft. Hood, Texas. They never discussed or rehearsed a peaceful entry. Eighty members of the Bureau were trained in advanced commando tactics by Army Special Forces. Agents had begun practicing an armed assault in Waco as early as August, 1992, working within 150 yards of the Davidian auto business.

In July of 1992, Davy Aguilera, the agent in charge of the Waco investigation, visited licensed gun dealer Henry McMahon for an unannounced compliance check. McMahon had legally sold some 100 weapons to Koresh. After inspecting his books, Aguilera began to question McMahon about these purchases. Walking into the next room, McMahon telephoned David to inform him. Koresh responded, "If there's a problem, tell them to come out here. If they want to see my guns, they're more than welcome." McMahon told the agents that David was on the phone and inviting them to visit Mt. Carmel. According to McMahon, Aguilera nervously began shaking his head and whispering, "No, no!"

McMahon had met David Koresh in the spring of 1991. He remembered him as an inspired and persistent biblical enthusiast, who was demonstrably fond of kids. He described the children as happy, well-adjusted, intelligent, well-cared-for, and trusting of adults. David explained that he was buying firearms for investment purposes. He believed their value would increase, a prophetic assessment. He and McMahon formed a partnership, legally assembling AR-15 rifles for sale at gun shows. The parts were purchased by McMahon, and stored at Mt. Carmel. The Davidians provided financing and labor. The parts ran about $400. An assembled rifle sold for $600. After the 1994 inaccurately titled "Assault Weapons Ban," the price jumped to $1400.

PREVIOUS EVIDENCE OF COOPERATION WITH AUTHORITIES. A cordial relationship had long existed between the Branch Davidians and the local police. David Koresh had never been convicted of a crime, violent or otherwise. The community had complied with law enforcement several times. In 1987, following a bizarre incident with a former leader of the sect, Koresh and seven others were peaceably arrested, charged with attempted murder, tried, found not guilty, and released. Years later, David did not interfere with a Michigan judge's decision to remove a 12-year-old child from the sect. And in February of 1992, he personally escorted the local sheriff and a state investigator on a tour of Mt. Carmel, after they called to say they were coming to look into allegations of child-abuse by former members.

FLAWED AFFIDAVIT FOR SEARCH AND ARREST WARRANTS. The initial charges against the Davidians were contained in an affidavit for a search warrant written by agent Aguilera. He alleged they were engaged in violating federal tax laws by converting semi-automatic weapons to fully-automatic status, and the making of grenades and explosive devices without a license. Despite intensive efforts, he failed to establish probable cause. The evidence was so technically flawed and sloppy that no warrant should ever have been issued.

Apparently aware of this, Aguilera's affidavit attempted to paint Koresh as an anti-Christ who must be stopped immediately at all costs. He alleged ominous deviations from moral norms, that fall well outside the jurisdiction of the ATF. He conjured imminent threats of apocalyptic dangers.

MARC BREAULT. The main source of most of these accusations was an embittered Australian ex-Branch Davidian, who, perhaps unwittingly, was the prime mover in the destruction of Mt. Carmel. He had lived with Koresh from 1988 to mid 1989. Initially an enthusiastic disciple, he turned against Koresh primarily because of David's evolving sexual doctrines and practices. Breault organized a virulent campaign with the help of his wife and other ex-disciples when he returned to Australia. He set himself up as a rival prophet. He contacted law enforcement agencies in the U.S. with complaints, approached U.S. government offices in Australia, and hired a private investigator to help coordinate these activities. An Australian TV host gave Breault's charges wide exposure.

The ATF flew Breault from Australia to California for an interview in January 1993 despite the fact that reliance on disaffected sect members is a poor investigative practice. They are known to be hostile and biased sources of information. Interestingly enough, the large number of ex-Branch Davidians suggests it was a simple matter to leave the group. Breault was quoted as a source by *The New York Times* every day for one week beginning the day after the raid. Since the *Times* is a major source of information for other news agencies, the public's hunger for knowledge of this unknown group was satisfied by Breault's uncorroborated poison. He was also a major source for the *Waco Tribune-Herald's* inflammatory seven-part series, the "Sinful Messiah."

THE BOTCHED ATF RAID. Agency spokespeople claimed after the failed assault that Koresh couldn't be peaceably arrested by himself because he had not left the compound for months. However, numerous local residents had seen him around town as early as six days before. He was a regular patron at the Chelsea Street Pub, which he visited once a week through mid-February. He was also a regular jogger whose runs extended beyond the Mt. Carmel property line.

Four undercover agents had moved across the street in January, posing as students at a local college. Their new clothes and expensive cars made Davidians suspicious. They checked with the college to learn the agents weren't students. One agent, Robert Rodriguez, became a regular visitor at Mt. Carmel. In both his trial testimony and an interview with *The Dallas Morning News* he stated that he never saw any illegal activity during a month of surveillance.

On the day of the raid, the Branch Davidians had nearly two

hour's advance warning. Editors at Dallas TV stations stated that an ATF public information officer called on Saturday seeking the weekend phone numbers of anchors because "something big" was going to happen on Sunday. Eleven reporters and three networks were on the scene of the raid, one from as far away as Oklahoma City. A TV cameraman was responsible for alerting the Davidians to the raid. Mt. Carmel resident David Jones stopped to offer help to a lost motorist, who excitedly informed him that agents prepared for a shootout were on their way. Jones rushed home to inform Koresh while agent Rodriguez was visiting. Rodriguez was allowed to leave peaceably.

After the failed raid, ATF Director Steven Higgins stated on *Face the Nation*, "Our agents walked into an ambush ... " Yet, Rodriguez had advised that the raid be called off when he knew it had lost the element of surprise. Although nearly one hundred agents rode up to the door of the church in two unprotected cattle transport vehicles, no shots were fired by Branch Davidians. If they were truly a hostile force, they would have mowed down the assault force before ATF agents could fire the first shot.

The raid was scheduled for late Sunday morning, when working people and school children would be at home. The agency claimed the scheduling of the raid had to be "moved up," because of the publication by the *Waco Tribune Herald* of its "Sinful Messiah" series. However, their warrants expired on February 28. No ambulances or fire vehicles were in the area. ATF was forced to commandeer news reporters' vehicles after agents had been shot during the attack. They did not use hard body armor though they claimed the "cult" was heavily armed.

They lied to Texas Governor Ann Richards to secure use of State National Guard helicopters by claiming drug manufacturing was taking place at Mt. Carmel. Before the ground assault began, three helicopters circled the compound firing through the wooden roof of the Davidian home. The helicopters received return fire. Yet ATF raid leaders neither halted the ground assault nor warned ground commanders of the additional danger. Helicopter fire was confirmed by the testimony of two lawyers who were allowed to visit their clients twice during the 51-day siege that followed the raid. Dick DeGuerin and Jack Zimmerman represented David Koresh and his right hand man Steve Schneider. Zimmerman stated he observed bullet exit holes in the second floor ceiling of the women and children's living quarters — indicating fire from above.

The firing of the first shot is a key issue. David Koresh claimed ATF fired first after he opened the front door. DeGuerin and Zimmerman believed he was telling the truth because they saw the two front doors peppered with incoming bullet holes. There would be no reason for the bullet holes to be in the door if ATF agents were firing at Davidian snipers in the windows, as they claimed. Nor would the number of bullet holes indicate controlled fire discipline. However, at the 1994 trial, it was learned that half of Mt. Carmel's double front door (steel and fireproof) was "missing" from evidence. Two ATF agents, as well as three Davidians, testified at the trial that ATF fired first. At least three of the six dead Davidians were unarmed.

THE STANDOFF. After the failed ATF raid, the FBI took charge of the scene. Initially it was hoped sect members would just surrender. They refused to do so, leading to an ill-coordinated FBI strategy combining negotiation and tactical force. Koresh might make a concession to the negotiating team. Then, a punishing activity would be pursued by the tactical group. When David would renege on his promise, FBI spokesmen would tell the media what a bad guy he was. Special Agent in Charge Jeffrey Jamar repeatedly found it expedient to publicly mock the sect's religious beliefs, and David Koresh's leadership, during the tightly controlled, and one-sided, daily news media briefings. He also insisted he was dealing with a "hostage situation," despite the fact that every one of the 14 adults who left the residence by their own choice during the standoff expressed both loyalty and devotion to David.

Ron Engelman, a popular talk show host, arranged a communication code with the Davidians after phone lines were cut by the FBI. They requested Engelman's help to get medical assistance for their wounded, and a negotiator to help with authorities. Koresh agreed to surrender if doctors were allowed to care for the wounded. The FBI refused and later played back the tapes of the conversation on a loudspeaker to taunt him. Engelman bitterly complained that withholding medical assistance for the wounded was more severe treatment than used against the Viet Cong.

"PSYCHOLOGICAL OPERATIONS." The FBI instituted a program of mental torture beginning on March 14, in an attempt to force the Davidians to surrender. The worst effect of these torments was undoubtedly on the children. Tactics included the following.

- Bright spotlights aimed into the residence throughout the night.
- Ear splitting recordings of whining and taunting voices, dentist drills, rabbits being slaughtered, Tibetan monks chanting, and Nancy Sinatra singing her famous line "... one of these days you know you're gonna get burnt."
- Targeting specific automobiles for destruction by tanks.
- Smashing children's toys that had been left outside.

Dr. Alan Stone of Harvard University, a lawyer, psychiatrist, and nationally recognized expert on violence, wrote that the FBI conduct was a "... misguided and punishing law enforcement strategy that contributed to the tragic ending ..." The brutal psychological tactics and heavy show of force were warned against early on by FBI behavioral scientists, who claimed this would only enhance apocalyptic mentality. They proposed a more conciliatory approach to negotiation.

THE CULT BUSTERS. The public was continually prepared for a violent end to the standoff by endless appearances on television, major magazines and newspapers by Cult Awareness Network personnel and other "expert deprogrammers." These psycho-fascists interpret any religious behavior or belief outside the secular norm as indicative of "cult-based mind control." Professional cult-busters, hired by FBI siege leaders, were described by the media as "negotiators," "consultants," and "advisers." Among them was Rick Ross, a convicted jewel thief and embezzler. Ross had recently been assessed $2.5 million in punitive damages by a federal jury in Seattle for his part in the 1991 kidnapping and "deprogramming" of a young fundamentalist. The jury found him, and Cult Awareness Network, guilty of violating the young man's right to freedom of religion. Total damages in the case were nearly $5 million.

THE FIRE. The siege against surviving Branch Davidians ended with the fiery deaths of 21 children and 53 adults broadcast live on national television. The FBI had chosen to terminate negotiations. Bob Ricks, FBI spokesman, said at 10:30 am on April 19, "We're saying come out ... this matter is over." Two hours later it was. FBI began forcibly inserting canisters of CS gas with tanks, smashing through the fragile wooden walls of Mt. Carmel. The CS gas, used against women and children in Waco, is banned for use in battlefields under the Chemical Weapons Convention. It causes dizziness, disorientation, shortness of breath, chest tightness, nausea, burning of the skin, intense tearing, coughing and vomiting. The children would have been the most harmed because of their smaller size. While some Davidians had gas masks for relief, these masks do not fit children.

The video footage shows such violent ramming of the building that it must be seen to be believed. The structure was simply demolished. Falling debris blocked a trap door to an underground shelter, killing those inside. A front stairway collapsed, leaving the women's and children's second-floor exit cut off. The roof over the gymnasium collapsed, killing others in that area. The main entrance and exit doors in front were blocked.

Around noon, the building caught fire. I recorded the following entry in my diary. "It is 4:30 p.m. on April 19, 1993. To the best of my knowledge the Branch Davidians in Waco, Texas are dead. The news broadcast which I saw live on NBC stated that upon firing into the compound to make openings for the tear gas, the building caught fire. About half an hour later, the Justice Department stated that two members of the group had been observed setting fire to the compound at either end. I am writing this to make clear that it contradicted the live broadcast."

The fire was the worst disaster in U.S. law enforcement history. The federal and media spin doctors were at work immediately. They had their work cut out for them. At 6:11 that morning, the FBI had called Parkland Hospital in Dallas to check how many beds were available in the burn unit. Yet they made no provisions for water trucks or fire-fighting equipment. After the fire started, FBI agents waited 10 minutes before calling the fire department, then held them for 16 minutes after they arrived on the scene. Described by the media and the government as a "fortress," the building was a tinderbox constructed mostly from used lumber and plywood. It burned to the ground in a mere 45 minutes.

CAUSE OF THE FIRE. According to lawyers Zimmerman and DeGuerin, the cause of the fire was either a lantern or propane bottle being knocked over by a tank, or the CS gas spontaneously igniting. The FBI had cut off electricity to the building on March 12. They knew the Davidians were relying on gasoline powered generators, kerosene lamps and propane fuel, and that they had piled bales of hay for protection against bullets.

FEDERAL CHARACTER ASSASSINATION. After the fire, President Clinton wasted no time in calling the Branch Davidians a "bunch of fanatics [who] decided to kill themselves . . ." He said of David Koresh, "[His] response to the demands for his surrender . . . was to destroy himself and murder the children who were his captives as well as the other people who were there . . ." And, just to make sure no one felt too badly about the deaths of so many people at the hands of his administration, Clinton added, "We know that David Koresh had sex with children."

Regarding allegations of mass suicide, however, former FBI head William Sessions stated April 20th on *The MacNeil-Lehrer News Hour*, that "every single analysis made of his [Koresh's] writing, of what he had said, of what he said to his lawyers, of what behavioral science people said, what the psychologists thought, the psycholinguists thought, what the psychiatrists believed, was that this man was not suicidal." Koresh had been working on a manuscript, had discussed publication rights with his lawyer Dick DeGuerin, and had retained a literary agent. He had asked DeGuerin to help prepare a will to protect Davidian property rights, and establish a trust fund for the children to safeguard future income from media sales. Steve Schneider was even concerned about whether he should get a haircut before the surrender.

CHILD ABUSE. Both DeGuerin and Zimmerman believed that the charges of child abuse were part of a purposeful disinformation campaign spread by the ATF, the FBI, the Justice Department, and the White House. Zimmerman was adamant that there was no evidence of child abuse. He said the children were, "well-fed, they were clean and they were well-adjusted. They smiled, they talked to us . . ." A home-made video filmed by the Davidians during the siege surfaced some time after the fire. Small children are seen affectionately climbing on David and playing with him, further contradicting the accusations of child abuse. The footage was purposely withheld from the public by the government during the standoff, lest it engender sympathy for the group.

A near fantasy level of child abuse charges were parroted by an uncritical media. James Tom, for example, claimed that Koresh spanked Tom's 8-month-old daughter for 30 to 40 minutes until she was bleeding; and that Tom didn't try to stop it because he might get hurt. He claimed to have immediately recognized Koresh as a

Charles Manson figure, and said David wanted one of Tom's children for a human sacrifice. No reporter bothered to ask why, given this presumably astute assessment, Tom willingly enrolled himself and his family under such leadership.

Janet Reno claimed that child abuse initially brought the Davidians to the attention of the feds, despite the fact that child abuse is under state, not federal, jurisdiction. Reno further said that child abuse was the basis for the original raid, and that her decision to smash holes in the walls with tanks and insert CS gas was caused by her "information that infants were being slapped around and beaten." Later she admitted she couldn't exactly *prove* this "in terms of a criminal case." She claimed that this statement was a misunderstanding of something someone (she forgot who) had told her. Later still, she admitted she did not read the FBI's prepared statement carefully, nor did she read the supporting documentation assembled for her review prior to authorizing the final assault. On April 21, the Justice Department acknowledged that there was no evidence of child abuse during the standoff (despite the electronic surveillance) but that psychiatrists were speculating that with Koresh under pressure *there must have been!*

The Texas Department of Protective and Regulatory services issued a case summary on April 23, 1993 stating that the former allegations of child abuse could not be verified by their previous investigation; that no additional charges had been filed since the investigation closed the year before; and that no evidence of child abuse was provided by examining or interviewing the 21 children released during the 51-day siege.

ARSON INVESTIGATION. The government hired an arson investigator named Paul Gray who "confirmed" that Davidians used gasoline to set the April 19 fire. Gray is the husband of an ATF employee in its Houston office, and was a friend of one of the dead agents. Gray's office had been located in the ATF Houston office from 1982 to 1990. He carried an ATF identification card. Jack Zimmerman said, "We're the only ones that were on the inside, saw the physical evidence, talked to the people inside who are now dead, and also talked to the survivors. That bullshit story about the way the fire started was put out by that ATF agent disguised as a Houston Fire Department officer."

DESTRUCTION OF EVIDENCE. The continuous moving, plowing, and shifting around of the crime scene destroyed evidence of shell casings, which would have proved who fired what, and how much of it, during the raid. Crushing the cars destroyed trajectory data, as did smashing the bullet-hole-ridden walls of the house with tanks. The fire destroyed more evidence. On May 12, government officials simply bulldozed the burned-out ruins. Assistant US Attorney in Waco, William Johnston, complained in a March 23 letter to Janet Reno that Jeffrey Jamar was destroying evidence about the ATF raid. Johnston was removed from the case. During the trial, Texas Rangers complained that FBI agents were loading trash into a dumpster as Rangers were attempting to process the crime scene for evidence.

GOVERNMENT THIEVERY. Thousands of dollars worth of automobile tools disappeared from the Mag Bag garage when it was ransacked by agents. The FBI smashed through the garage doors with tanks on March 8, even though the landlord offered them keys. A church safe containing more than $50,000 in cash, plus personal valuables of church members, was signed over to the FBI by Texas Rangers. It was not on the evidence list prepared by the government. The government attempted to seize the 77-acre Mt. Carmel land, described as "prime ranch property."

THE TRIAL. Eleven surviving Davidians faced their day in court beginning in January 1994. The 10 count indictment included conspiracy to murder federal agents, murder of federal agents, and various federal firearm violations. The government sought to win life sentences against all defendants with the conspiracy to murder charges, since three of them were not even present at Mt. Carmel on the day of the ATF raid.

THE VERDICT. All eleven Branch Davidians were found not guilty of conspiracy to commit murder, and of aiding and abetting in the murders of the four ATF agents. The New York Times called the verdict "a resounding warning against the use of excessive force by law enforcement." The jury deliberated for three days. Three Davidians were found not guilty of all charges. Eight others were found guilty of lesser charges, including aiding and abetting voluntary manslaughter and various weapons possession counts.

The jury, however, made an unfortunate technical error. They misunderstood one of the charges. They found seven Davidians guilty of the charge in Count Three of the indictment, "using and carrying a firearm during and in relation to the commission of an offense." This charge was linked to Count One, "conspiracy to commit murder." The legal error was that since there was no *conspiracy to murder*, defendants could not be guilty of carrying weapons to commit *conspiracy to murder*.

Judge Smith gave a long and audible sigh when he read this part of the verdict and called the defense and prosecution attorneys to the bench. The prosecution urged the Judge to return the count to the jury for a better-informed assessment. The defense urged him to just throw it out as a misunderstanding.

JUDGE OVERTURNS VERDICT. Smith adjourned the proceeding for the weekend after releasing two of the Davidians who had been cleared of all charges. On Monday, February 28, 1994, the first anniversary of the ATF raid, he released a third defendant, Ruth Riddle, who had been convicted solely of the Count Three charge. However, under pressure from the prosecution, he reversed himself and had her re-arrested. He next declared that even though all Davidians had been found innocent of the conspiracy to murder charge in Count One, the fact that the jury (mistakenly) found seven of them guilty of the weapons charge in Count Three *proved* that they were in fact guilty of the conspiracy to murder charge in Count One!

The jurors were horrified and made public pronouncements of their sorrow at their error, and their disagreement with the Judge. Jury foreman Sara Bain told Smith in a letter that the jury had misunderstood the charge. If Count Three were returned, they would find the defendants not guilty. The much-maligned Branch Davidians were now suffering an abandonment of the Constitutional protection of trial by jury.

SENTENCING. Smith next extrapolated various technical loopholes so that he was able to sentence five Davidians to an additional 30 years each for the Count Three conviction. The foreman of the jury cried on the steps of the courthouse, lamenting that the judge had simply overlooked the jury's verdict. The Davidians were to serve a combined total of 240 years. The jury had convicted them of charges which would have given them 70 years maximum. The Judge added

170 years to their sentences by finding them guilty of crimes the jury had acquitted them of committing. In June, 2000, the Supreme Court remanded the case for re-sentencing, and Smith was forced to reduce the sentences of the five members from 30 to five years for the Count Three charge, and to reduce the sentence of a sixth defendant by five years.

EVOLUTION OF A POLICE STATE. Waco has been characterized as the confrontation between a maniac claiming to be the Son of God, and a tyrannical Federal Government convinced that it is God. The first World Trade center bombing preceded the ATF attack by two days. The two incidents prompted a show on Ted Koppel's *Nightline* favoring additional restrictions on the First and Second Amendments, especially when combined. Koppel's question was: Are the First and Second Amendments outdated in "complex" modern society? (Ironically, the Clinton administration's refusal to treat the World Trade Center bombing as seriously as it did "domestic extremists," would arguably set the stage for the September 11, 2001 attacks.) As the ATF triumphantly raised its flag over the ashes of Mt. Carmel, the American flag might well have hidden her beauty in sorrow.

GUN CONTROL. The Branch Davidians were accused of being a "heavily armed cult" by nearly every Establishment media source in early 1993. The truth was far more benign. Texas Rangers recovered about 200 guns from the ashes, or about two guns per adult resident. Statewide in Texas the average is four guns per adult. Approximately 16,500 Texans own automatic weapons. One quarter million Americans were registered owners of machine guns in 1993. If semiautomatic firearms had been converted to fully automatic fire by the Branch Davidians, the crime consisted of not registering the converted weapons, and not paying the $200 federal tax on their possession. Whatever one's views of the Second Amendment, 86 people dead over a $200 gun registration tax is insane.

FREEDOM OF RELIGION. Statism is the mortal enemy of idealism. When the ultimate source of authority and morality is the state, God becomes an antiquated and dangerous adversary. Since the fall of the Soviet Union, the new enemy is religious fundamentalism, whether Islamic, Jewish or Christian. It is beyond doubt that David Koresh held strange religious beliefs. But neither he nor any other Branch

Davidian ever forcibly interfered with anyone else's right to believe as they chose.

THE LONELINESS OF THE BRANCH DAVIDIANS. Richard A. Schweder of the University of Chicago wrote an Op-Ed piece published in *The New York Times* on April 17, 1994.

> [N]o one stepped forward to be the Davidians' friend. The ATF spent months planning and rehearsing the largest "law enforce-ment" operation of its 200-year history. This turned out to be a major military operation worthy of a police state, carried out against the domestic residence of an unpopular and readily stig-matized religious community. The American Civil Liberties Union does not like guns, and it's very busy, so it didn't get involved. The religious leaders of our country do not like "cults," and the women's movement does not like patriarchal living arrangements, so they didn't much care. And no one wanted to seem sympathetic to "child abuse" or unsympathetic to the FBI. Throughout the 51-day standoff, an uncharacteristic silence fell across the editorial pages of many leading newspapers.

DENOUEMENT. A series of Congressional hearings finally took place in July and August of 1995, soon after officials were awakened to the seriousness of continued public discontent by the Oklahoma City bombing. The Congressional hearings determined that the April 19 fire was set by the Davidians. However, during the hearings, evidence was presented of FLIR (Forward Looking Infra-Red) or heat-sensitive video footage taken by government surveillance planes on the day of the fire. It appeared that government operatives were firing auto-matic weapons into the cafeteria at the rear of the burning building, well out of sight of the carefully positioned cameras of the media. (All reporters and camera people were kept some three miles away throughout the siege.) As shocking as it was, this video footage was not addressed in depth at the hearings because of various levels of confusion.

In 1998, Waco documentary producer Mike McNulty discov-ered government issued military pyrotechnic munitions in a locked FBI evidence storage facility. This caused another uproar that forced Janet Reno in 1999 to appoint former Senator John Danforth as a special counsel to investigate this discovery, revisit the FLIR evidence, and review the presence of Army Special Forces personnel at Waco in violation of the Posse Comitatus Act. To no one's surprise Danforth concluded in his November 2000 report that despite the FLIR evidence, government agents did not gun down Branch Davidians trying to escape the fire by running out the back of the building. Danforth also confirmed that, despite the discovery of the pyrotechnic shells, the Davidians had set the fire themselves. And finally, he reported that elite military personnel were present solely in an advisory capacity.

My advice to any reader troubled by the horrific possibilities raised in the preceding two paragraphs is to purchase the videos *Waco: The Rules of Engagement* and *Waco: A New Revelation*, both by Mike McNulty, and draw your own conclusions. (Please order as suggested in Recommended Reading to avoid poorly edited version.)

In July of 2003, I visited the Branch Davidian Church with my family and two friends to pay our respects. Our shared first impression was that the accusation these people were planning to swarm into Waco to attack others was simply insane. The isolation of their land spoke volumes about their lifestyles and intentions. Miraculously, the community has managed to avoid the land grab many felt, in part, helped motivate the attack. Donations have come in from all parts of the world to help sustain the property. A beautiful arbor of 82 trees commemorates each of the Davidians who died. A humble new church graces the land. A core group of about six survivors, who now live off-site, continue their devotions, joined by new members. Foreign born Davidians were repatriated. Other survivors drifted away. Imprisoned Davidians continue serving their unjust sentences. The wrongful death lawsuit, initially filed by family members in 1994, alleging excessive use of force by the U.S. government, was dismissed in September of 2000.

As if a grim replay of the untimely deaths of the three chief co-conspirators responsible for the fiery deaths of the Knights Templar in 1314, several key players in the Waco drama also fared rather ill. President Clinton was disgraced by becoming the second president in American history to be impeached; Janet Reno was savaged by Parkinson's disease; and J. Michael Bradford, the U.S. attorney who successfully defended the government in the wrongful death lawsuit mentioned above, committed suicide in 2003.

The new Branch Davidian Church and a view of the memorial arbor, both built with contributions received from well wishers throughout the world. BELOW: The beautiful sentiments expressed on this monument hardly sound like the frothings of homicidal cop killers. (Photos by Frank Sottile © 2003)

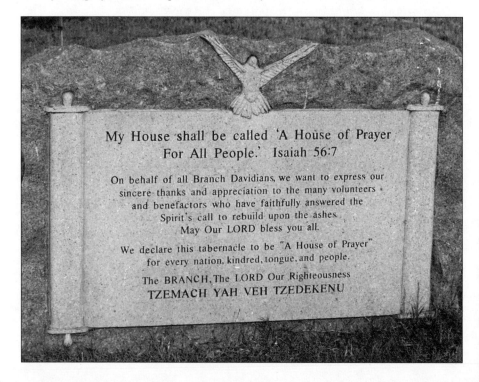

My House shall be called 'A House of Prayer For All People.' Isaiah 56:7

On behalf of all Branch Davidians, we want to express our sincere thanks and appreciation to the many volunteers and benefactors who have faithfully answered the Spirit's call to rebuild upon the ashes. May Our LORD bless you all.

We declare this tabernacle to be "A House of Prayer" for every nation, kindred, tongue, and people.

The BRANCH, The LORD Our Righteousness TZEMACH YAH VEH TZEDEKENU

SEPTEMBER 11, 2001
REMEMBERED

The Koran is our constitution, the Prophet is our Guide. Death for the Glory of Allah is our greatest ambition.
— Slogan of the Muslim Brotherhood

The judgment to kill and fight Americans and their allies, whether civilian or military, is an obligation for every Muslim who is able to do so in any country.
— *Fatwa* issued by Osama bin Laden in 1998

The companion volume to this book, *The Templars and the Assassins: The Militia of Heaven*, came off press on May 15, 2001. During that summer, I began work on its projected sequel, *The Divine Warrior*, an elaboration of the themes studied earlier over a wider range of cultures. The horrific events of September 11, 2001 particularly shocked me because the methods and organizational structure employed by the Sunni Muslim terrorists against America were reminiscent of those used by the Shiite Muslim Assassins.[1] People sought my opinion on the modern activities of the Islamic terror network. I was forced to confront my rather clear admiration of Hasan-i-Sabah, founder of the group.

Hasan was the first leader to maximize the technique of selective political murder for the advancement and defense of the interests of his community. During his reign in northern Persia from 1095 until 1135, Hasan is known to have arranged for the deaths of 50 strategically chosen individuals. The word "Assassin," common to many European languages, is derived from this sect.

---

[1] After the Prophet Muhammad's death in 632, a council of elders appointed his father-in-law, Abu Bakr, as the first Caliph or defender of the faith. The caliph is the political and religious leader of the Muslim theocratic state. He is not viewed as a new Prophet, rather he is the protector of orthodoxy.

A minority group supported Muhammad's cousin and son-in-law, Ali, as the natural leader of Islam, because of his ties of blood to the Prophet, especially through his marriage with Fatima, Muhammad's sole surviving offspring. Those who accepted the caliphate of Abu Bakr are known as Sunnis. The dissenters who supported Ali are the Shiites.

Almost all of the political activities of the medieval Assassins were directed against the policy makers with whom they disagreed, and who actively threatened their survival. Initiates of all spiritual traditions share a basic respect for human life. I would propose that Hasan-i-Sabah and his successors were living examples of that respect. In fact, I praised them in my earlier book for pursuing a more humane approach to the vicissitudes of politics through their policy of targeting opposing leaders. Traditional warfare involves untold numbers of soldiers and civilians killed in support of their leaders' policies. This opinion may seem naive in view of the fundamentalist nature of Hasan-i-Sabah's beliefs, however, it is, at least, not contradicted by the facts of the historical record.

Osama bin Laden, and the Islamic fundamentalist terror network he represents, have an altogether different approach. Despite what I am certain is bin Laden's sense of Hasan as a forerunner, the modern Islamic terrorist has no respect for human life, and little concern for the spiritual consequences of random murder of innocent people including fellow Muslims. Like the medieval Assassins, they seek maximum intimidation of their enemies. However, unlike the Assassins, they kill wantonly. Certainly there is a legitimate comparison to be made between the genius and organizational models of the two men. Bin Laden's technological tool kit was far greater than that available to Hasan-i-Sabah. With satellite phones, Apple computers, fax machines, and air travel, bin Laden was able to build a multinational organization which Hasan might admire.

The modern media world of images also presents an effective forum for the type of campaign waged by al-Qaeda and allied groups. No one can state with certainty whether Hasan-i-Sabah, were he alive today, might not adopt these methods too. However, again turning to the historical record, the Mongols and many others mentioned in *The Templars and the Assassins*, demonstrated a ruthless and indiscriminate murderous ferocity in their campaigns. Hasan, like Archimedes, seemed to have understood the physics of carefully applied force achieving maximum results. He also seems to have been acutely aware of the spiritual consequences of taking life.

* * *

In order to be able to view the modern Middle East struggle in a context wider than this morning's headline, a reading of the Old

Testament and the Koran will yield enormous perspective. The tribal conflicts over which the modern world grieves with such energy have been going on for at least 5000 years.

Militant Islam is equal parts revolutionary political movement and fundamentalist religious revivalism. It is a movement that transcends the boundaries of the state. Language barriers and national identities recede before the declared unity of religious belief and sense of the destined mission of Islam. For centuries after the coming of the Prophet, Islam was a unified cultural/religious/political entity that knew no national boundaries, besides those of various clans or tribes who reigned over specific regions. For some thirteen centuries Islam was ruled by the Caliphate. The division of the people of the Middle East into modern nation states is a development less than a century old, dating to the fall of the Ottoman Empire in 1918. Nor was it an organic cultural/political evolution. On the contrary, it was a construction imposed by European imperialists, primarily French and British, who drew maps and insisted their drawings were reality.

The modern Islamic terrorist movement burst into world attention on September 5, 1972 with the Black September murders of Israeli athletes during the Munich Olympics. However, this action, taken under the Marxist PLO banner, was secular and atheistic at its core, a nationalist political protest against the Israeli state, decorated with the bangles of religion to draw in the weak-minded.

The establishment of the Iranian revolution in 1979, on the other hand, heralded the emergence of the fundamentalist Muslim state and the proclamation of religious *Jihad* (Holy War) against the unbeliever and infidel. Ayatollah Khomenii, the Shiite leader of Iran (Persia), must be seen in some measure as a true successor to Hasan-i-Sabah. He was able to organize a band of powerless, stateless, religious rebels into a group capable of overtaking one of the most powerful and well-oiled military machines of the Middle East.

Khomenii also accomplished something that Hasan did not. That was the union of fundamentalist Shiites with fundamentalist Sunnis. From this singular accomplishment was born the modern Islamic terrorist network, in large part directed or coordinated from Tehran. A thousand year old dream was realized. The primacy of, and alliances between, Hizballah, the Iranian controlled Shiite terror master network, and the Wahhabi controlled Sunni Hamas is evidence of Khomenii's achievement.

The most common rationale for Islamic violence is generally

expressed as U.S. support for Israel. However, the roots of the fundamentalist Sunni movement extend considerably further back in
time. The *Salafiyya*, or community of True Believers (a broad term
for Islamic fundamentalists), look back to the first three generations
of Muslims (the *salaf* or "forerunners," the pious ancestors who followed Muhammad) for their inspiration.

Islamic orthodoxy, as a theme among the Sunnis, may be traced
at least to Ahmad ibn Hanbal (780–855). He was the leader of the
most strict of the four schools of Islamic jurisprudence. He compiled
the Traditions of the Prophet. He was persecuted by the Abassid
caliph after he refused to accede to a secular, rationalist interpretation of the Koran that declared reason the equivalent of revelation.
His courageous martyrdom at the hands of his persecutors has earned
him the undying respect of religious Muslims for over a millennium.

The medieval theologian Ibn Taymiyah (1263–1328) is another inspiration to both orthodox Muslims and the Islamo-fascists who
appear to be holding Islam hostage. Taymiyah was a member of the
Pietist school founded by Hanbal. He endured imprisonment and
persecution by secular-minded Muslim leaders because he too refused
to bend his traditionalist, orthodox view of the Koran as the inspired
word of Allah. Under attack, he increased his preaching efforts, and
died in prison. He has been quoted as an authority in bin Laden's
propaganda efforts.

The Templars and the Assassins described in great detail the
extreme convolutions in the development of Islam, and the charac-
teristic tension between religion and politics that is the result of its
theocratic nature. It is important to understand that the orthodoxy
for which ibn Hanbal and ibn Taymiyah were martyred is a common
element in the religious heritage of the larger Muslim community.
They are respected as teachers and philosophers, spiritual guides, and
examples of religious purity to the faithful.

In contrast, the beginning of what we know today as Islamo-
fascism, or the Islamist movement, has its roots in the eighteenth
century — when religion and politics were joined as a hammer to be
wielded by an armed state against its population.

It began with Muhammad ibn Abd al Wahab (1703–1792) who
preached a return to the ways of the Prophet. He gazed back to Ibn
Taymiyah for inspiration. Wahab first began to preach against the
Sufis and their broad-based tolerance and spiritual creativity. His
message was a humorless, puritanical search for an orthodox glory

that would reclaim the elevated past of Islam. He condemned the use of tobacco, the worship of saints, and the decoration of mosques. Al-Wahab's message of fundamentalist reform was embraced by the House of Saud in 1744, in the person of tribal leader Muhammad ibn Saud. Wahhabi Saudis ransacked the Shiite holy city of Karbala in 1801. Saud first conquered Mecca in 1806. His descendants finally succeeded in establishing — and continue to rule — modern Saudi Arabia. Wahhabiism is the official state religion. Its massive outreach and conversion efforts are funded by the seemingly inexhaustible wealth of the oil-rich Saudi kingdom.

During the 19th century, a series of anti-colonialist protests flourished throughout much of the Arab world. Most decried the increased secularization taking place through the renewed contact with Europeans, and lamented the overall sense of failure of Islamic culture in the modern world. They preached that the technological weakness of the Muslim culture was a consequence of the abandonment of the tenets of Islam. Meanwhile the House of Saud continued to strive toward control of the entire Arabian peninsula. Arabia was largely exempt from the colonial efforts of Europe, because oil had not yet become an issue.

In the 20th century, the religious fundamentalist/political movement raised the banner of the Muslim Brotherhood (*Ikhwan al-Muslimun*) in Egypt in 1931. The Brotherhood was founded by Hassan al-Banna (1906–1949) who may have been the first modern Muslim to introduce "a corrosive hatred of the Jews, which he seemed to have adopted from Nazism."[2]

The most illustrious spokesman of the Muslim Brotherhood was Sayyid Qutb (1906–66). He had committed the Koran to memory at age 10, yet received a modern college education in Cairo. His embrace of fundamentalist activism was stimulated, in part, by a trip to the U.S. in 1948. He participated in a study mission organized by his employer, the Egyptian Ministry of Education. He was revolted by the materialism and sexual promiscuity he observed, as well as by American support for the state of Israel, founded a year earlier. He returned to Egypt in 1951 and became involved with the coup which elevated Gamal Abdel Nasser to the rulership of Egypt. He was disappointed by the Marxist direction of Nasser's Pan Arabic movement, envisioning instead a society based on the Koran. As editor of

---

[2] Steven Schwartz, *The Two Faces of Islam*, Doubleday, New York, 2002, p 129.

the journal of the Muslim Brotherhood, Qutb became the primary philosophic voice of the Islamist movement in the Arab world. When Nasser achieved power, he betrayed his Islamist allies and Qutb was imprisoned. Qutb survived torture and a decade of abhorrent prison conditions. He smuggled his writings out of prison, including his massive commentary on the Koran, citing its passages from memory. His proselytizing activities finally led to his execution by Egyptian authorities. The brilliance and eloquence of his writing attracted many followers, as did the example of his martyrdom to his ideals.

Hasan al-Turabi, the leader of Sudan's National Islamic Front, is an important disciple of Sayyid Qutb, and a crucial intellectual/spiritual influence on Osama bin Laden. A graduate of the Sorbonne, al-Turabi sought to create the ideal Islamic state in Sudan. He seized power through a military coup in 1989 and imposed a Sunni fundamentalist regime with his ally President Omar Bashir. He organized the Islamic Peoples Congresses, held semi-annually from 1991 to 1996, during which bin Laden was able to expand his network by meeting with the illustrious assembled militant leaders from terrorist groups throughout the Muslim world.[3]

Abdullah Azzam (b. 1941) was another major influence on bin Laden, whom he met in 1978. As a young man, Azzam's studies took him to Cairo where he formed close connections to the family of Sayyid Qutb and the Muslim Brotherhood. He worked tirelessly to build an international Islamic network, and to provide a conduit for funds, supplies, and personnel from Saudi Arabia to the Afghan *mujahideen* or "holy warriors," who fought the 1979 Soviet takeover of their country. Azzam declared that support for the efforts of the *mujahideen* was the obligation of every Muslim. He was a charismatic and persuasive orator, who recruited and inspired thousands of jihadists.

Sayyid Qutb was also a major intellectual influence in the life of Ayman al-Zawahiri, the brilliant Egyptian physician and radical co-

---

[3] According to Sudan's ambassador to the UN, Sudan made an offer to the U.S. in 1996 to arrest bin Laden and turn him over to U.S. custody. This offer was made, in part, because of a power struggle between al-Bashir and al-Turabi. Al-Bashir was desperate to end Sudan's isolation, and the economic sanctions imposed on the country because of its overt support for terrorism, encouraged by al-Turabi's policies. For further details on this, and much else of note, please see *Losing Bin Laden*, Richard Miniter, Regnery Publishing, Inc., Washington D.C., 2003.

leader of al-Qaeda, who has been another major influence on bin Laden. He founded the highly secret Jihad group in Egypt in 1973 as the radical arm of the semi-public Islamic Group, founded a decade earlier. Sheikh Omar Abdel Rahman (the blind cleric, imprisoned at the time of this writing for his role in the first World Trade Center bombing) was the spiritual leader of both groups. In 1981, they accomplished the assassination of Anwar Sadat, the president of Egypt. Al-Zawahiri was imprisoned for three years. He later traveled to Pakistan and Afghanistan to help the *mujahideen* against the Soviets. Descended from a wealthy family, he is well-educated with an excellent command of English. Despite his status as a known terrorist, he made two trips to America in the mid 1990s for fundraising efforts among American Muslims.

Osama bin Laden joined the Muslim Brotherhood as a university student in the late 1970s. His first contact with Afghanistan came at the age of 23. He was sent to Peshawar, Pakistan, near the Afghan border, as an envoy of Prince Turki bin Faisal, the chief of Saudi intelligence during most of the Afghan war. Their friendship was built on a shared concern for the decline and decadence of modern Islamic regimes. The Afghan war against the Soviet empire was bin Laden's introduction to the armed conflict of militant Islam with the infidel. When the *mujahideen* won after a decade of struggle (in large part because of help from the U.S.), and the Soviet empire fell soon after, they felt empowered and unstoppable.[4]

Bin Laden's radicalization continued through the eighties. He formed al-Qaeda ("the Base") in 1988, in order to expand the militant Islamic movement beyond Afghanistan. A decisive chapter in his evolution came after Saddam Hussein's 1990 invasion of Kuwait. The Saudi government begged America for help, and allowed American and European military forces to establish bases on Saudi soil. This enraged bin Laden because the sacred lands of Arabia, particu-

---

[4] America's support of the *mujahideen* as a proxy army in the battle with Soviet communism, after the Soviets invaded Afghanistan in 1979, made a great deal of sense. Our abandonment of these allies at the moment of their victory, has been the source of much hatred. It was a consummate act of diplomatic stupidity to allow the lawless, poverty-ridden, economically-destroyed, infrastructure-empty, heavily-armed society to fall to the control of criminal gangs. These were actually brought under control by the rise to power of the Taliban government, which restored a measure of order to the country. The Taliban embraced bin Laden (in part) because of his financial generosity.

larly the areas around and between Mecca and Medina, are forbidden to any non-Muslim by long tradition dating back to the Prophet. The real climax came after Saddam's army was forced out of Kuwait in 1991. The Western bases and their godless forces were allowed to remain on Muslim holy soil. Bin Laden turned into an implacable foe of the Saudi royal family, and was expelled from the kingdom in 1994.[5]

* * *

Despite the Crusades, and the nineteenth and twentieth century colonialist meddling and betrayals by Europeans and Americans, Muslim culture itself bears the primary responsibility for its current predicament. When one looks deeper into the rage of the so-called "Arab Street," it becomes increasingly clear that we are dealing with the politics of frustration and envy. According to World Bank estimates, the total exports of the entire Arab world — excluding oil — amount to less than those of Finland.[6] While uncounted trillions of dollars have flown into the coffers of the oil producing lands, the majority of people live in squalor. Extremists scream colonial oppression. However, what Jihadists call "rape of resources" might be termed "commerce" by another culture.

The corrupt Arab oligarchies, who control both the vast oil revenues of the region, and the protection money paid as foreign aid by the West, are to blame for the poverty and unemployment that fuel the rage of Arab people. The greed and corruption of many modern Islamic rulers follows on the lack of good judgement, and poor organizational skills of their immediate predecessors. Muslim countries that became independent of Western colonial rulership after World War II often embraced the failed political and economic system of socialism in their attempt to modernize. This is understandable because of the dictatorial models of their historic governments. Traditionally, Muslim rulers commanded by unchallenged fiat, bolstered

---

[5] The end of the first Gulf War was the occasion of an even more bizarre betrayal of Islam by the U.S. than our abandonment of the *mujahideen*. After the war, George Bush the Elder, called upon the Iraqi Shiites and Kurds to rise up against Saddam Hussein. When they bravely answered his call, Bush totally abandoned them. Tens of thousands of Iraqis were ruthlessly slaughtered and a great deal more hatred was directed against America.

[6] *What Went Wrong*, Bernard Lewis, Oxford University Press, NY, 2002, p. 47.

by both religion and wealth. However, in the modern world, the net effect of attempting to upgrade Arab economies by central planning and bloated bureaucracies was to maintain these countries as poverty stricken, third-world hovels. When countries like Egypt and Syria became client states of the Soviet empire — the embodiment of godless materialism — fundamentalists were further alienated.

The disparity between the oil revenues of the ruling class, and the economic hardship of the masses, motivated cynical regimes, like the Saudis, to encourage the rise and spread of Wahhabi extremism. The purpose of their support is twofold. One is as a form of hush money to mitigate against the rhetoric of the Islamists. The second is a practical program to export their domestic troublemakers elsewhere. Muslim governments are hard-pressed to crack down appropriately on jihadist violence, as they are justifiably afraid of being perceived as the very enemies of Islam the Jihadists paint them to be.

The pool of resources that feeds Islamo-fascism begins in the Wahhabi supported *madrassa* schools. The religious school system began in the Middle Ages as a series of Koranic academies to regularize the Sunni faith and combat heresy. However, under Wahhabi control, a large percentage of modern *madrassas* function as pressure cookers for a kind of jingoistic madness composed of hatred and irrationalism. As one example, some students are taught to accept that the world is flat — because it was so pronounced by Sheikh Abdel Aziz al Baz, rector of the University of Medina, as recently as the 1960s. *Madrassa* graduates may be able to recite portions of the Koran by rote, but they are likely to be functionally illiterate, and unsuited for any employment besides jihad. Robin Wright discusses the difficulties faced by some Muslim parents in fighting the teachings to which their children are exposed. Unlike Arab Nationalism or Socialism, with which one might argue at the family dinner table, criticizing the distorted teaching of a mullah may be considered anti-Islamic apostasy.[7] As discussed elsewhere in this book, the possibilities of indoctrination offered by a widely-based school system create enormous opportunities for social manipulation.

* * *

[7] Robin Wright, *Sacred Rage: The Wrath of Militant Islam*, Simon & Schuster, New York, 2001, p. 130.

The overall goal of the Islamist movement is the establishment of a Caliphate, a pan-Islamic government spanning all countries in which Muslims reside. At this moment, the first goal is control of the Mideast countries. Next, are plans to expand as far east as the Philippines. The long range goal is world domination. Like the Internationalist vision of global government superceding national sovereignty, the Jihadist movement seeks dissolution of national boundaries and the erection of a Muslim super state — a world in which all nations and all peoples live under *Sharia*, the Muslim rules of religious, social, and political governance.

The massive Muslim immigration into Europe and the United States may well help to provide a foothold for that dream. Eighty percent of American mosques are controlled by Wahhabi Imams, according to Hisham-al-Kabbani, head of the Islamic Supreme Council of America.[8] Most Muslims living in the West are undoubtedly not interested in following these pernicious teachings. However, the mosque system allows financial sponsors to pick their own clergy. And the Saudi Wahhabis have a lot of money to spend. Therefore, despite whatever disagreement a Muslim may have with the political goals of the Jihadists, they are the ones controlling the flow of religious information to the community. Furthermore, like all successful conspirators, Islamo-fascists are patient.

They recognize that ambitious Muslims — those who brave relocation to America in search of better living conditions, and who are willing to work hard to advance themselves in their new homeland — will be the least responsive to fundamentalist distractions. But there are the children. The very parents who are striving to better their children's fates are subject to manipulation by propagandists for the cultural hegemony of their Islamic roots. Add to this the left wing domestic magpie chorus hymning its litany of "diversity," and the result is that Muslim immigrant parents are stuck between the proverbial rock and a hard place. They are scarcely encouraged to adopt the values of their new country, when both their own religious leaders, and a divisive cultural gestalt scream for separatism.

The "average" Muslim is also in as great a danger as the more vocally identified enemies of the Jihadists. Moderate Muslims throughout the world are perceived as embracing the hated cultural

[8] *The Two Faces of Islam*, Steven Schwartz, p. 240.

products of the West — television, music, computers, the Internet, automobiles, and a relaxation of fundamentalist morality. They are frequently the victims of Islamo-fascist fury — in defiance of the Koran — as demonstrated by the substantial number of Muslim casualties in terrorist attacks worldwide. The Islamo-fascists realize that decent, rational, courageous Muslims are their greatest enemies — as well as mainstream Islam's greatest hope of defeating the appropriation of the faith.

* * *

I would suggest that America needs to face several realities. First is that the enemy here is not only serious, but determined and bloodthirsty. His sense of justification for his grievances reaches 1300 years into the past. Gazing back to the time of the Prophet, the extremist Muslim has not advanced much further than the Islamic world view of the twelfth century. To maintain that kind of hostility through the centuries is pathological. There will be no negotiation with this enemy.[9] The continuous stream of hatred of the West, expressed by the Islamists, includes constant references to the Crusades. Bin Laden's umbrella organization, founded in 1998, is called the World Islamic Front for Jihad Against Jews and Crusaders.

Bin Laden is neither a modern day Robin Hood, nor an Islamic David pursued by a Judaeo-Christian Goliath, nor some latter day James Dean rebel *with* a cause hunted by the most powerful nation on earth. One might more accurately characterize him as a combination between Cotton Mather and Jerry Falwell. His Maid Marions would be covered from head to foot in *burquas* (restrictive apparel in no wise sanctioned by the Prophet). Bin Laden expressed his admiration for the Taliban state as one approaching his ideal of the proper Muslim political structure. Afghanistan, under the Taliban, was an Orwellian Religious Police State, whose bureaucracy included a Ministry for the Promotion of Virtue and the Prevention of Vice. Machine-gun wielding fanatics zooming around in Japanese pickup trucks — like a caricature of Charlie Manson's fevered hallucinations of the Dune Buggy Attack Brigade — beating, torturing and killing those who violated their insanely restrictive puritanical codes

---

[9] In further support of this assertion, please see *The Letter to the Terrorists* that follows this essay.

— hardly a latter day band of Merry Men. Note well: All the compassion and understanding in the world will merely result in allowing this enemy to approach close enough to slit your throat.

Let us also keep in mind that, like all our other Wars on Nouns (Drugs, Poverty, Illiteracy, Hunger, *ad nauseum*), the War on Terror is bound to fail unless we pursue it as a serious matter of survival — neither a video game nor a think-tank discussion. The worried faces we see on TV need to be ignored. Bin Laden's greatest mistake may have been in assuming that President Bush's reaction to September 11 could be extrapolated from an observation of his predecessor, who spent much of his administration ignoring the mounting threat of militant Islam, and the balance pursuing ineffectual responses.[10]

I hope al-Qaeda and allied Islamo-fascists will have years to regret that assumption. More importantly, I hope that both President Bush and his successors in office will be able to distinguish between America's citizens and America's enemies. If American society self-destructs by erecting a totalitarian, surveillance-based police state, the Islamist opponent will be one step closer to his goal. The tyrant lives in greatest fear of the individual. His entire apparatus is designed to destroy that single unit. It is much easier to change the doctrine of a society than it is to change the culture. America is still struggling to maintain its culture of individualism. If we succumb as a culture to the herd mentality, it will merely take a more powerful manipulator to redefine the specifics of the herd's "thinking."

On a more positive note, al-Qaeda's attack on America has caused a renewal of something long lost in the post-Vietnam cultural depression that has so sorely afflicted American society during most of my lifetime. Courage, militarism, patriotism, and honor are virtues that have been scorned for nearly forty years. Many Ameri-

---

[10] See *Losing Bin Laden*, by Richard Miniter, and *Bin Laden: The Man Who Declared War on America*, by Yossef Bodansky, Random House, NY, 1999, 2001. The Clinton administration refused to see the first World Trade Center bombing on February 26, 1993 as a matter of national security, viewing it instead as a law enforcement problem and humanitarian disaster. Clinton never even bothered to visit the site of over 1000 casualties including seven deaths, and millions of dollars in damage. The ill-handled investigation did not reveal the connection between the operation's director Ramzi Yousef (nephew of al-Qaeda commander Khalid Sheikh Mohammed) and Osama bin Laden until 1995. (In my opinion, Clinton was more concerned with domestic "anti-government extremists." The ATF raid against the Branch Davidians occurred just two days after the first World Trade Center attack.)

cans are again openly acknowledging that a strong military, decisive national self-interest, and a spirit of appreciation for our unique American freedoms are long overdue. The concept of the self-reliant citizen-soldier, upon which this country was founded, is another idea worth revisiting. The government couldn't protect us on September 11, 2001, nor will it be able to always protect us. While bureaucratic vigilance is necessary in a sane society, personal vigilance is the key. When firearms training joins driver education in America's high schools, we will be a freer and safer society.

* * *

Those who come to our shores must again be encouraged to become un-hyphenated Americans. Theodore Roosevelt eloquently discussed this issue during the great wave of European immigration in the early years of the twentieth century.[11]

> There is no room in this country for hyphenated Americanism. When I refer to hyphenated Americans, I do not refer to naturalized Americans. Some of the very best Americans I have ever known were naturalized Americans, Americans born abroad. But a hyphenated American is not an American at all.... Americanism is a matter of the spirit and of the soul. Our allegiance must be purely to the United States. We must unsparingly condemn any man who holds any other allegiance. But if he is heartily and singly loyal to this Republic, then no matter where he was born, he is just as good an American as any one else.
>
> The one absolutely certain way of bringing this nation to ruin, of preventing all possibility of its continuing to be a nation at all, would be to permit it to become a tangle of squabbling nationalities, an intricate knot of German-Americans, Irish-Americans, English-Americans, French-Americans, Scandinavian-Americans or Italian-Americans, each preserving its separate nationality, each at heart feeling more sympathy with Europeans of that nationality, than with the other citizens of the American Republic.

[11] Theodore Roosevelt 1915 quoted in Philip Davis (ed.), *Immigration and Americanization* (Boston: Ginn and Company, 1920), available at http://www.rpatrick.com/USA/americanism/

Respecting cultural roots allows people to contribute a rich fiber that may be woven into the tapestry of American society. But people in this country, and those who come to live in this country, must share a common ideology in order for America to remain a nation.[12] America's unique national doctrine is based on the acceptance of the premise that we are endowed by our Creator with certain unalienable rights — and these rights include individual liberty, the rule of law, private property, and the consent of the governed.

The modern world is being offered a false choice between two equally obnoxious futures: the first is the secular, statist tyranny of the Internationalist camp; the second is the theocratic, statist tyranny of the Islamo-fascist network. I firmly believe that our uniquely American concepts of "life, liberty and the pursuit of happiness" offer a political alternative that can triumph in the world of ideas — if we are brave enough to live by them.

---

[12] I fully understand that the immigration floodgates have been opened by those American leaders who hate our nation's ideology, and equally despise the very concept of nationhood.

LETTER TO THE TERRORISTS

Copies of the following letter were found in the effects of three of the September 11 hijackers, the original in the possession of operation commander Muhammad Atta. The author is unknown. It was translated by Imad Musa of the Capital Communications Group in Washington D.C., and is reproduced here with their kind permission.

When I first read this, soon after the September 11 attacks, I was struck by two things. The first was the utter seriousness of the state of meditative concentration enjoined upon the hijackers. This was no idle group of unemployed Palestinian teenagers or mentally addled shoe bombers. These men were professionals, and they were deeply instructed in the disciplines of their faith. I was also struck by the similarity between this letter and that written during the Crusades by St. Bernard of Clairvaux to Hughes de Payens in 1135, outlining the proper behavior and spiritual frame of mind expected of the dedicated Templar knight/monk. A new translation of that letter, by Lisa Coffin, was published four months before the attack in *The Templars and the Assassins: The Militia of Heaven.*

When presidential hopeful Al Sharpton stated in an October, 2003 campaign debate that today's terrorist is tomorrow's friend, I realized he probably hadn't read this letter. The timeless and cosmic proportions of the antagonism this enemy harbors will not be assuaged by anyone's charming rhetoric. This is a battle between cultures that has been raging for centuries.

One irony here is that some of the 9/11 hijackers spent their last nights in strip clubs drinking alcohol, which is forbidden to observant Muslims. Terrorists linked to al-Qaeda in the Philippines were also reportedly consuming alcohol, frequenting nightclubs, and sexually amusing themselves during their time in Manila. I remain unclear whether this was an attempt to invoke cover, a spiritual failing on the part of nervous aspirants, or, more likely, further proof that politics continues to make for strange bedfellows. Does the religious fundamentalism of the Islamist network provide an employment veil for a criminal and secular revolutionary auxiliary of Islamo-fascists, more concerned with fascism than Islam?

I have taken the liberty below of interspersing portions of St. Bernard's nine-century-old letter (distinguished by italic type) with the letter written by the unknown spiritual leader of the September 11 killers.

The Last Night[1]

1. Making an oath to die and renew your intentions.
   Shave excess hair from the body and wear cologne. Shower.
2. Make sure you know all aspects of the plan well, and expect the response, or a reaction, from the enemy.
3. Read *al-Tawba* and *Anfal* [traditional war chapters from the Qur'an] and reflect on their meanings and remember all of the things that God has promised for the martyrs.

This new order of knights is one that is unknown by the ages. They fight two wars, one against adversaries of flesh and blood, and another against a spiritual army of wickedness in the heavens.

4. Remind your soul to listen and obey [all divine orders] and remember that you will face decisive situations that might prevent you from one hundred percent obedience, so tame your soul, purify it, convince it, make it understand, and incite it. God said: "Obey God and His Messenger, and do not fight amongst yourselves or else you will fail. And be patient, for God is with the patient."

Dedicated all together, they are of one heart and one soul: in this manner no one follows his own individual will, but yields to a leader. Neither do they idly shirk their official obligation, nor wander aimlessly.

5. Pray during the night and be persistent in asking God to give you victory, control and conquest, and that He may make your task easier and not expose us.
6. Remember God frequently, and the best way to do it is to read the Holy Qur'an, according to all scholars, as far as I know. It is enough for us that it [the Qur'an] are the words of the Creator of the Earth and the plants, the One that you will meet [on the Day of Judgment].
7. Purify your soul from all unclean things. Completely forget something called "this world" [or "this life"]. The time for play is over

---

[1] All comments in editorial brackets in the text of the letter are those of Mr. Musa.

and the serious time is upon us. How much time have we wasted in our lives? Shouldn't we take advantage of these last hours to offer good deeds and obedience?

8. You should feel complete tranquility, because the time between you and your marriage [in heaven] is very short. Afterwards begins the happy life, where God is satisfied with you, and eternal bliss "in the company of the prophets, the companions, the martyrs and the good people, who are all good company." Ask God for his mercy and be optimistic, because [the Prophet], peace be upon him, (used to prefer optimism in all his affairs).

O life is secure, where conscience is chaste! Life is secure for those who anticipate death without fear, and, on the contrary, desire it greatly with passion and embrace it with devotion!

9. Keep in mind that, if you fall into hardship, how will you act and how will you remain steadfast and remember that you will return to God and remember that anything that happens to you could never be avoided, and what did not happen to you could never have happened to you. This test from Almighty God is to raise your level [levels of heaven] and erase your sins. And be sure that it is a matter of moments, which will then pass, God willing, so blessed are those who win the great reward of God. Almighty God said: "Did you think you could go to heaven before God knows whom amongst you have fought for Him and are patient?"

But in truth the knights of Christ may fight securely in battle for their Lord, and by no means fear either sin if they slay the enemy, or the danger of their own death. Because either to bring about death, or to die for Christ, you have not sin but an abundant right to glory. No matter which the case, Christ wins, for in the first case he willingly accepts the death of the enemy, and in the second freely gives consolation to his knight.

10. Remember the words of Almighty God: "You were looking to the battle before you engaged in it, and now you see it with your own two eyes." Remember: "How many small groups beat big groups by the will of God." And His words: "If God gives you victory, no one can beat you. And if He betrays you, who can

give you victory without Him? So the faithful put their trust in God."

They rush in to attack the adversaries, considering them like sheep. No matter how outnumbered, they do not consider the savage barbarians as formidable multitudes. Not that they are secure in their own abilities, but they trust in the virtue of the Lord Sabaoth to bring them to victory.

11. Remind yourself of the supplications and of your brethren and ponder their meanings. (The morning and evening supplications, and the supplications of [entering] a town, and the [unclear] supplications, and the supplications said before meeting the enemy.)
12. Bless your body with some verses of the Qur'an [done by reading verses into one's hands and then rubbing the hands over things over whatever is to be blessed], the luggage, clothes, the knife, your personal effects, your ID, your passport, and all of your papers.

Truly, he is a fearless knight and completely secure. While his body is properly armed for these circumstances, his soul is also clothed with the armor of faith.

13. Check your weapon before you leave and long before you leave. (You must make your knife sharp and you must not discomfort your animal during the slaughter).[2]
14. Tighten your clothes [a reference to one making sure his clothes will cover his private parts at all times], since this is the way of the pious generations after the Prophet. They would tighten their clothes before battle. Tighten your shoes well, wear socks so that your feet will be solidly in your shoes. All of these are worldly things [that humans can do to control their fate, although God decrees what will work and what won't] and the rest is left to God, the best One to depend on.
15. Pray the morning prayer in a group and ponder the great rewards of that prayer. Make supplications afterwards, and do not leave your apartment unless you have performed ablution before leav-

[2] Tomorrow's friend indeed!

ing, because (The angels will ask for your forgiveness as long as you are in a state of ablution, and will pray for you). This saying of the Prophet was mentioned by An-Nawawi in his book, *The Best of Supplications*. Read the words of God: "Did you think that We created you for no reason . . ." from the Al-Mu'minun Chapter.

When readying for imminent battle, their inner faith is their pro-
tection. . . . They seek victory, not glory. They would rather
strike terror than impress. They are not violent men, and do not
thoughtlessly or frivolously rush about, but exercise skilled con-
sideration. With caution and prudence they set themselves in
military order, accordingly to the ancient scripture: "Truly
Israelites are men of peace, even when they rise up to make
war."

THE SECOND STEP:

When the taxi takes you to (M) [this initial could stand for *matar*, airport in Arabic] remember God constantly while in the car. (Remember the supplication for entering a car, for entering a town, the supplication of place and other supplications).

When you have reached (M) and have left the taxi, say a supplication of place ["Oh Lord, I ask you for the best of this place, and ask you to protect me from its evils"], and everywhere you go say that prayer and smile and be calm, for God is with the believers. And the angels protect you without you feeling anything. Say this supplication: "God is more dear than all of His creation." And say: "Oh Lord, protect me from them as You wish." And say: "Oh Lord, take your anger out on them [the enemy] and we ask You to protect us from their evils." And say: "Oh Lord, block their vision from in front of them, so that they may not see." And say: "God is all we need, He is the best to rely upon." Remember God's words: "Those to whom the people said, 'The people have gathered to get you, so fear them,' but that only increased their faith and they said, God is all we need, He is the best to rely upon."

Secured, therefore, advance you knights and drive away the ene-
mies of the cross of Christ with an untroubled soul. Be certain

that neither death nor life has the power to separate you from the
grace of God, in whom is Christ Jesus. Indeed at every kind of
danger reply, "Whether we are to live or whether we are to die,
we are the Lord's."

After you say that, you will find [unclear] as God promised this
to his servants who say this supplication:

1) They will come back [from battle] with God's blessings
2) They were not harmed
3) And God was satisfied with them.

God says: "They came back with God's blessings, they were not
harmed, and God was satisfied with them, and God is ever-blessing."
     All of their equipment and gates and technology will not pre-
vent, nor harm, except by God's will.[3] The believers do not fear such
things. The only ones that fear it are the allies of Satan, who are the
brothers of the devil. They have become their allies, God save us, for
fear is a great form of worship, and the only one worthy of it is God.
He is the only one who deserves it. He said in the verses: "This is
only the Devil scaring his allies" who are fascinated with Western
civilization, and have drank the love [of the West] like they drink
water [unclear] and have become afraid of their weak equipment "so
fear them not, and fear Me, if you are believers."

In the death of the pagan is Christian glory because Christ is
glorified.... I do not mean that pagans are to be slaughtered, if
there is another way to prevent them from their extraordinary ag-
gression and oppression of the faithful. It seems, however, more
gracious to slay them than to let them sin strongly, win over the
just, and therefore, perhaps the righteous will choose to take sin
into their hands.

Fear is a great worship. The allies of God do not offer such worship except for the one God, who controls everything. [unclear] with

---

[3] Homeland Security and Transportation Safety Administration, take note. Maybe
we can begin to fly like human beings and citizens again!

total certainty that God will weaken the schemes of the non-believers. God said: "God will weaken the schemes of the non-believers."

You must remember your brothers with all respect [?]. No one should notice that you are making the supplication, "There is no God but God," because if you say it one thousand times no one will be able to tell whether you are quiet or remember God. And among its miracles is what the Prophet, peace be upon him, said: (Whoever says, 'There is no God but God,' with all his heart, goes to heaven." The prophet, peace be upon him, said: (If you put all the worlds and universes on one side of the balance, and "No God but God" on the other, "No God but God" will weigh more heavily." You can repeat these words confidently, and this is just one of the strengths of these words. Whoever thinks deeply about these words will find that they have no dots [in the Arabic letter] and this is just one of its greatnesses, for words that have dots in them carry less weight than those that do not. And it is enough that these are the words of monotheism, which will make you steadfast in battle [unclear] as the prophet, peace be upon him, and his companions, and those who came after them, God willing, until the Day of Judgment.

Also, do not seem confused or show signs of nervous tension. Be happy, optimistic calm because you are heading for a deed that God loves and will accept [as a good deed]. It will be the day, God willing, you spend with the women of paradise.

> Smile in the face of hardship young man/
> For you are heading toward eternal paradise

The knight of Christ may strike with honor and perish with honor. For when he strikes he serves Christ, and when he perishes in Christ he serves himself. He does not carry a sword without just cause, for he is a minister of God, and he punishes malicious men for the praise of the truth. If he kills malicious men, he is not a murderer under these circumstances. I say that he is a murderer of wickedness and a champion of Christ. He drives away malicious men and is the defender of the Christian order. On the other hand if he is killed, he has not perished but has come home.

You must remember to make supplications wherever you go, and anytime you do anything, and God is with his faithful servants, He will protect them and make their tasks easier, and give them success and control, and victory, and everything.

THE THIRD PHASE:

When you ride the (T) [probably for *tayyara*, airplane in Arabic], before your foot steps in it, and before you enter it, you make a prayer and supplications. Remember that this is a battle for the sake of God. As the prophet, peace be upon him, said: (An action for the sake of God is better than all of what is in this world), or as he said. When you step inside the (T), and sit in your seat, begin with the known supplications that we have mentioned before. Be busy with the constant remembrance of God. God said: "Oh ye faithful, when you find the enemy be steadfast, and remember God constantly so that you may be successful." When the (T) moves, even slightly, toward (Q) [unknown reference], say the supplication of travel. Because you are traveling to Almighty God, so be attentive on this trip.

> Certainly, whether they die in bed or in war, the death of His sacred ones is precious without wavering in the eyes of the Lord; but to die in war how much more precious and glorious.

Then [unclear] and then it takes off. This is the moment that both groups come together. So remember God, as He said in His book: "Oh Lord, pour your patience upon us and make our feet steadfast and give us victory over the infidels." And His words: "And the only thing they said Lord, forgive our sins and excesses and make our feet steadfast and give us victory over the infidels." And His prophet said: "Oh Lord, You have revealed the book, You move the clouds, You gave us victory over the enemy, conquer them and give us victory over them." Give us victory and make the ground shake under their feet. Pray for yourself and all of your brothers that they may be victorious and hit their targets and [unclear] and ask God to grant you martyrdom facing the enemy, not running away from it, and for Him to grant you patience and the feeling that anything that happens to you is for Him.

> How glorious to return from the victories of such a battle! How blessed to die a martyr in battle! Rejoice, courageous champion,

if you live and conquer in the Lord, indeed there is great rejoic-
ing and glory. If you die, you are joined with your Lord. Life is
certainly fruitful and victory is glorious, but a sacred death is
truly more important. To be sure, if "they who die in the Lord
are blessed," how much more blessed are they who die for the
Lord?

Then every one of you should prepare to carry out his role in a
way that would satisfy God. You should clench your teeth, as the
pious early generations did.

When the confrontation begins, strike like champions who do
not want to go back to this world. Shout, "Allahu Akbar," because
this strikes fear in the hearts of the non-believers. God said: "Strike
above the neck, and strike at all of their extremities." Know that the
gardens of paradise are waiting for you in all their beauty, and the
women of paradise are waiting, calling out, "Come hither, friend of
God." They have dressed in their most beautiful clothing.

Let the swords of the faithful fall on the necks of the enemy in
order to destroy anyone who is himself against the knowledge of
God, by which is the faith of Christians, in order that the heathen
not say: "Where is their God?"

If God decrees that any of you are to slaughter, you should ded-
icate the slaughter to your fathers and [unclear], because you have
obligations toward them. Do not disagree, and obey. If you slaughter,
do not cause the discomfort of those you are killing, because this is
one of the practices of the prophet, peace be upon him. On one condition: that you do not become distracted by [unclear] and neglect
what is greater, paying attention to the enemy. That would be treason, and would do more damage than good. If this happens, the deed
at hand is more important than doing that, because the deed is an
obligation, and [the other thing] is optional. And an obligation has
priority over an option.

Do not seek revenge for yourself. Strike for God's sake. One time
Ali bin Abi Talib [a companion and close relative of the prophet
Muhammad], may God bless him, fought with a non-believer. The
non-believer spit on Ali, may God bless him. Ali [unclear] his sword,
but did not strike him. When the battle was over, the companions of
the prophet asked him why he had not smitten the non-believer. He

said, "After he spit at me, I was afraid that I would be striking at him in revenge for myself, so I lifted my sword." After he renewed his intentions, he went back and killed the man. This means that before you do anything, make sure that your soul is prepared to do everything for God only.

> It is not acceptable, however, whether dead or alive, victorious or vanquished, to be a murderer. Unfortunate victory is his who has destroyed a man, succumbed to vice, and indulged in vainglory; then wrath and pride are your master.

Then implement the way of the prophet in taking prisoners. Take prisoners and kill them. As Almighty God said: "No prophet should have prisoners until he has soaked the land with blood.[4] You want the bounties of this world [in exchange for prisoners] and God wants the other world [for you], and God is all-powerful, all-wise."

> For they have driven away the transgressors of divine law and secured just people in the truth. Likewise do they overthrow the heathen that love war, and slay those who create our consternation, and drive away the wicked people from the holy city of the Lord.

If everything goes well, every one of you should pat the other on the shoulder in confidence that (M) and (T) number (K). Remind your brothers that this act is for Almighty God. Do not confuse your brothers or distract them. He should give them glad tidings and make them calm, and remind them [of God] and encourage them. How beautiful it is for one to read God's words, such as: "And those who prefer the afterlife over this world should fight for the sake of God." And His words: "Do not suppose that those who are killed for the sake of God are dead; they are alive . . ." And others. Or they should sing songs to boost their morale, as the pious first generations did in the throes of battle, to bring calm, tranquility and joy to the hearts of his brothers.

> These men are appointed by God and searched out by his hand to the limits of the land; honorable men of Israel to guard faith-

---

[4] Again, please note the self-admitted utter ferocity of this opponent.

fully and protect vigilantly the tomb, which is the bed of the true
Solomon, each man with sword in hand, and skillfully trained to
battle.

Do not forget to take a bounty, even if it is a glass of water to
quench your thirst or that of your brothers, if possible. When the
hour of reality approaches, the zero hour, [unclear] and wholeheart-
edly welcome death for the sake of God. Always be remembering
God. Either end your life while praying, seconds before the target, or
make your last words: "There is no God but God, Muhammad is His
messenger".
Afterwards, we will all meet in the highest heaven, God willing.

Truly does he not fear death, but instead he longs for death. Why
should he have a fear for life or for death, when in Christ is to
live, and to die is to gain? He stands faithfully and with confi-
dence in the service of Christ; he greatly desires for release and
to be with Christ, the latter certainly a more gracious thing.

If you see the enemy as strong, remember the groups [that had
formed a coalition to fight the prophet Muhammad]. They were ten
thousand. Remember how God gave victory to his faithful servants.
God said: "When the faithful saw the groups, they said, this is what
God and the prophet promised, they said the truth. It only increased
their faith."

Certainly they are confident when they remember the words of
the Maccabees, "It is easy for a multitude to be driven away by
the hands of a few. It makes no difference in the sight of the God
of Heaven whether he sets them free by the hands of many or by
a select few, because victory in war is not the result of a large
army, and fortitude is from Heaven." We have seen one man in
hot pursuit put a thousand to flight, and two drive away ten
thousand.

And may the peace of God be upon the prophet.

Pulling Liberty's Teeth

*A well regulated Militia, being necessary to the security of a free
State, the right of the people to keep and bear Arms, shall not be
infringed.*
— Second Amendment of the Bill of Rights

An armed society is a polite society.
— Robert A. Heinlein, *Beyond This Horizon*

A "Million" Misinformed Moms

To paraphrase a famous gun-controller of old, May 14, 2000 is "a
date that will live in infamy." A group, variously estimated
between 50,000 and 250,000 mostly women, forewent the traditional family pleasures associated with the annual Mothers' Day holiday
to rally around TV personality and former K-mart spokeswoman
Rosie O'Donnell. She was accompanied by such well-known gun
confiscation luminaries as Diane Feinstein, Maxine Waters, and
Sarah Brady, all of whom spent the day expressing their contempt
for the aspirations of America's founders, and their disdain for law-
abiding Americans who believe in the Second Amendment. It was
the first time, to my knowledge, that a mass protest was aimed directly at the Bill of Rights.

Many of the "Moms" at the march were undoubtedly veterans
of the anti-war movement of the 60s and 70s, when the youthful
idealism of a generation was masterfully manipulated by the anti-
American Left. Now in middle-age, those who never woke up to the
assault on Liberty embodied by the Nanny State bared their teeth for
a direct attack against the hated "rich, white, slave-owning men"
who designed the greatest, most prosperous, and most free nation in
the history of the world. Camille Paglia described the March as "the
gun-control protest organized (as the major media is finally admit-
ting) by the sister-in-law of Hillary Clinton's longtime lawyer pal
and hatchet woman, surly Susan Thomases ..."[1] Surprised?

---

[1] Camille Paglia, *The Million Mom March: What a crock!* Salon.com, May 17, 2000.

THE SECOND AMENDMENT: AN INDIVIDUAL RIGHT

The "shot heard round the world" was fired during the first battle of the American Revolution on April 19, 1775. It was aimed at British soldiers seeking to enforce British gun control laws by confiscating weapons and gunpowder belonging to the citizens of Concord, Massachusetts. Both Dr. Joyce Lee Malcolm in *To Keep and Bear Arms* and Dr. Stephen P. Halbrook in *That Every Man Be Armed*[2] have provided prodigious, compelling and common sense scholarship to prove that the Second Amendment is a right possessed by the people. If the reader has any doubt of this, please refer to these two scholars. On the other hand, the text of the amendment itself, especially its phrase "the right of the people" may be considered indicative. See also similar use of the phrase "the people" in Amendments 1, 4, 9, and 10. Why do most anti-gunners accept that "the people" refers to the people in those four amendments, while insisting "the people" refers to the state governments in Amendment 2?

The passionate and brilliant writings and speeches collected in *The Federalist Papers, The Anti-Federalist Papers* and *The Debate on the Constitution,* establish beyond a shadow of a doubt that the right of the individual American to keep and bear arms was one of the most important arguments brought forth in favor of the plan to consolidate the American Republic.[3] The words of the early leaders of America eloquently expressed their view that an armed populace is: 1) a natural check against tyranny, 2) the first line of defense against enemy attack, 3) the most competently equipped to enjoy the long-cherished common law right of self-defense, and 4) a natural force for the good ordering of society. At least 8 of the original 13 states had provisions in their constitutions that included recognition of the right of private citizens to keep and bear arms. The founders well understood that the liberties acknowledged and guaranteed by the Bill of Rights could only be held by a citizenry willing and able to protect its freedom, by force if necessary, from those who would attempt to seize it. The Second Amendment is *Liberty's Teeth.*

[2] Joyce Lee Malcolm, *To Keep and Bear Arms,* Harvard University Press, 1994, and Stephen P. Halbrook, *That Every Man Be Armed,* The Independent Institute, 1994.
[3] See The *Federalist Papers,* edited by Clinton Rossiter, Penguin Books, *The Anti-Federalist Papers and the Constitutional Convention Debates,* edited by Ralph Ketcham, Penguin Books, *The Debate on the Constitution,* (two volumes) edited by Bernard Bailyn, The Library of America.

Tyranny: Merely an Eighteenth Century Concern?

In 1787, Noah Webster wrote,

> Before a standing army can rule, the people must be disarmed; as they are in almost every kingdom of Europe. The supreme power in America cannot enforce unjust laws by the sword; because the whole body of the people are armed, and constitute a force superior to any bands of regular troops that can be, on any pretense, raised in the United States.[4]

When William Clinton was sworn into office for his first term, he warmly remembered his former professor at Georgetown University, Carroll Quigley, who may well have helped shape some of the attitudes toward the Second Amendment held by arguably the most anti-gun (and generally anti-individual rights) president in American history. Quigley wrote the following in his brilliant 1966 tome *Tragedy and Hope*.

> In a period of specialist weapons the minority who have such weapons can usually force the majority who lack them to obey; thus a period of specialist weapons tends to give rise to a period of minority rule and authoritarian government. But a period of amateur weapons is a period in which all men are roughly equal in military power, a majority can compel a minority to yield, and majority rule or even democratic government tends to rise.[5]

Much later in the book Quigley added the following.

> At the present time, there seems to be little reason to doubt that the specialist weapons of today will continue to dominate the military picture into the foreseeable future. If so, there is little reason to doubt that authoritarian rather than democratic political regimes will dominate the world into the same foreseeable future.[6]

[4] A *Citizen of America*, Philadelphia, October 17, 1787, quoted in *The Debate on the Constitution*, Part One p. 155.
[5] Carroll Quigley, *Tragedy and Hope*, Macmillan, 1966, p. 34.
[6] *Ibid*, pp. 1200-1201.

Undeterred by this nightmarish conclusion, Quigley quickly displays the confidence in alternate solutions and concern for the "quality of life" that undoubtedly touched the heart of his young protégé, "A period that is not democratic in its political structure is not necessarily bad, and may well be one in which people can live a rich and full social or intellectual life whose value may be even more significant than a democratic political or military structure."[7]

OVERTURNING THE CONSTITUTION

The civilian disarmament movement is working relentlessly to avoid the one legal means of enacting gun control — namely to amend the Constitution to either repeal the Second Amendment or to legally modify it. No lovers of the limitations on government imposed by the Constitution, gun control zealots are well aware of the obstacles placed in the path of "reformers" who seek to change it. A two-thirds majority of Congress may propose amendments which must then be adopted by three-fourths of the states. Even with these protections, such idiotic anomalies as Prohibition will occur. However this is not the concern of the civilian disarmament crowd. They seek to bypass the Constitution altogether.

As Jaime Sneider, wrote,[8]

[T]he language of organizers and supporters of the Million Mom March hints at a growing trend ... The (generally left-leaning) disgruntled individuals who have failed politically in getting gun-control measures passed have come to support Constitutional Nullification. . . . Perhaps the scariest thing about the gun-control movement is that they want to blur the existence of truth itself. According to their own words, gun-control leaders will not stop until the private ownership of guns is illegal and the Constitution overthrown. As such, they encourage nullification of the universal moral truths contained within that document. As the gun-control activists pursue their agenda by any means necessary — supporting ever larger and more intrusive government — the true

[7] *Ibid*, p. 1201.
[8] Jaime Sneider, *Columbia Daily Spectator* as reported by the *National Review* on May 15, 2000, *Taking Aim at The Constitution*.

ethical purpose of the Second Amendment will only become more apparent.

The following news report is especially instructive in that regard.

> United Nations Secretary-General Kofi Annan has called on the international community to stem the proliferation of small arms across the world. He told a special meeting of the Security Council that restricting the flow of such weapons would be a key challenge in preventing conflict in the next century. Estimates of the number of firearms in the world range from 100 million to 500 million. Mr. Annan said there was "no single tool of conflict so widespread, so easily available, and so difficult to restrict, as small arms." ... In his report Mr. Annan recommended that member states should: *Adopt gun control laws including a prohibition of unrestricted trade and private ownership of small arms.* [emphasis added][9]

Ask yourself whether this can be interpreted as anything other than an open call to overturn the U.S. Constitution and the Second Amendment in favor of so-called "international law."

GUN CONTROL AND AMERICAN CULTURE

On the day of the march, an estimated *20,000 gun laws* were on the books in America. To quote Ms. Paglia again,

> The Million Moms would do much more for this country if they would focus on the breakdown of family and community ties that produce sociopaths like the goons who shoot up schools and daycare centers. It was parental irresponsibility and neglect, and not simply the availability of guns, that were ultimately at the root of the Columbine massacre, where home-barbecue propane tanks had been converted into bombs.

Klebold and Harris spent one year planning their actions. In addition to illegally acquiring firearms, (and thereby violating some

[9] BBC Online News Network, Saturday, September 25, 1999.

twenty federal and state firearms laws) they deployed ninety bombs at the school, which, fortunately, failed to detonate.

The "Moms" might also have consulted the 1994 report of the rabidly anti-gun Janet Reno Justice Department, *Urban Delinquency and Substance Abuse: Initial Findings — Research Summary*.[10] Boys who own legal firearms were found to have the lowest rate of adolescent delinquency and drug use when compared to both those owning illegal guns, and those owning none.

Adolescent Group	Street crimes	Gun crimes	Drug Use
Non gun owners	24%	1%	15%
Illegal gun owners	74%	24%	14%
Legal gun owners	14%	0% (zero)	13%

The study attributed the disparity in part to the "socialization into gun ownership," of boys with their fathers who owned guns for hunting and sport. One might suppose the close parental bonding would be equally salutary for young girl shooters as well.

CREATING PUBLIC OPINION

The American public is fed a daily dose of cooked statistics in a manner reminiscent of George Orwell's novel *1984*. However, the tragic consequences of this propaganda on national policy threaten real life and real people. The general willingness of the American population to believe the lies of politicians and media spin-meisters, and the lack of interest in alternative news sources, are disturbing. An informed electorate can make decisions. A brainwashed mass merely regurgitates its conditioning.

Geoffrey Dickens, Senior Analyst of the respected Media Research Center, detailed his group's two-year study of the treatment of gun related issues by four evening news shows[11] (ABC's *World*

[10] Discussed by Robert W. Lee in *The New American* for April 24, 2000.
[11] Geoffrey Dickens, "Outgunned: How the Network News Media Are Spinning the Gun Control Debate," *The American Rifleman*, April 2000.

News Tonight, CBS *Evening News*, CNN's *The World Today*, and NBC's *Nightly News*) and three morning broadcasts (ABC's *Good Morning America*, CBS's *This Morning*, and NBC's *Today*). The study tracked these shows from July 1, 1997 to June 30, 1999.

The criteria for categorization of stories as either "anti-gun" or "pro-gun" were the following. Anti-gun statements were defined as ideas like "violent crimes occur because of guns," and "gun control prevents crime." Pro gun statements included ideas such as "criminals, not guns, cause crime," "Americans have a constitutional right to keep and bear arms," and "concealed carry laws help reduce crime." If such statements in a news reports were weighted in a ratio of at least 1.5 to 1, the story or segment was identified as either anti-gun or pro-gun. If the ratio was less than 1.5 to 1, the story was regarded as neutral.

In 653 network gun policy stories, the study found that stories advocating more gun control outnumbered stories opposing gun control by 357 to 36, or nearly **10 to 1** (260 were categorized as neutral). Anti-gun sound bites were twice as frequent as those with a pro-gun message, 412 to 209. Gun control advocates appeared on morning shows more than twice as often as pro gun voices (82 times compared with 37 times for gun rights advocates and 58 appearances by neutral spokesmen. Three hundred evening news segments were rated as follows: 164 anti-gun, 20 pro-gun, and 116 neutral. Talking heads were gun control advocates by 2 to 1. Of 353 gun policy segments on morning news shows, anti-gun stories outnumbered pro-gun by 193 to 15 or **13 to 1** (with 145 categorized as neutral).

In January 2002, a school shooting took place at the Appalachian School of Law in Virginia. A failing student killed three and wounded three. According to the media, the killer was "subdued" by fellow students. In reality, the fellow student ran to his car, grabbed his pistol, and confronted the killer with his drawn gun. At which point, the killer dropped his weapon and surrendered. Of the 280 news stories reporting that incident, only four mentioned that the deadly attack had been stopped by a student armed with a handgun.[12] Had law-abiding students and faculty been legally able to carry weapons, the assailant could have been stopped even sooner.

---

[12] *Guns, Freedom, and Terrorism*, Wayne LaPierre, WND Books, Nashville, 2003, p. 76, quoting the results of a LexusNexus news search on the shooting.

A FAMILIAR HALF-DOZEN ANTI-GUN LIES

1. The "Dead Children" Lie

In the words of David Kopel, "A full listing of the lies told by the antigun lobby could fill a book."[13] Perhaps the most egregious of such is the Myth of the Dead Children. How many days go by each week when some government hack or media newsreader doesn't bow his or her head and solemnly intone the figures of 13, 15, 17 or more children killed every day by guns. Our minds are forced to conjure images of over a hundred children a week lying dead, like little well-fed Biafrans in front of Daddy's bloody night stand.

In truth, the per-capita number of fatal gun accidents among children is at its lowest level since 1903, when these statistics started being kept. Furthermore, the actual number of child firearm fatalities is declining every year, even as the numbers of people with firearms in their homes increases. By way of example, in 1995, there were 1400 accidental firearm deaths in America, of which 30 involved children four and under, while 170 involved the five to fourteen age bracket, thus 200 children in total. (In 1999, that number fell to 88.)[14] By comparison 2900 children died in motor vehicles, 950 died by drowning, and 1000 died by fire and burns. More children die in bicycle accidents each year than by firearms.[15] Nobody wants even one child to die. Reducing firearm accidents even further is the goal of the NRA's brilliant Eddie Eagle Program, a common sense and effective firearm safety educational effort that has reached sixteen million children since 1988 — and has been boycotted, ignored, and slandered by the gun banners.

The mournful statistical mantra of the mass media/civilian disarmament lobby are cynically based on counting young adults as children. Thus a teenage gangland street-corner slaying; a young fleeing felon shot by a police officer after robbing a liquor store; a jealous 21-year-old shooting his wife's seducer in a bar; or a crack deal gone bad, are all counted as "children who die by firearms." Accidents are a part of life and cannot be regulated away. But it is important to

[13] David Kopel, Research Director of the Independence Institute, *National Review* April 17, 2000, *An Army of Gun Lies.*
[14] *Guns, Freedom, and Terrorism*, p. 173.
[15] John Lott, Jr. , *More Guns, Less Crime*, Chicago, University of Chicago Press, 1998, p. 9.

note the utter shamelessness with which these statistics are manipulated to provide fodder for those seeking to expand the range of government control.

2. The "Guns Cause Crime" Lie

"Normal" people do not turn into crazed maniacs when a gun is
placed in their hands, any more than guns levitate from tables, pock-
ets, holsters, or closets to discharge themselves and kill innocent
people. The oft-repeated statement that a gun in the home is 43
times more likely to kill a family member than a criminal is another
purposeful distortion of the truth to serve a political agenda. "Of the
43 deaths, 37 are suicides; and while there are obviously many ways
in which a person can commit suicide, only a gun allows a small
woman a realistic opportunity to defend herself at a distance from a
large male predator."[16]

Another of the big lies of the gun control lobby is that most
people are killed by people they know. This argument is concocted
from the FBI Uniform Crime Report which states that family killings
account for 18% of murders, while 40% were committed by those
who "knew" their victims. The category of "those who knew their
victim" however, includes drug dealers and buyers, prostitutes and
clients, cab drivers killed by passengers, rival gang members involved
in turf wars, and murderous barroom brawlers.

Perhaps a more telling statistic is that in 1988, over 89% of adult
murderers had adult criminal records.[17] A 1996 study of youthful
homicide arrests found that 75 percent of youthful killers in Min-
nesota had been arrested at least once, with an average of 7.8 arrests
each. In Massachusetts, 77 percent of the young people arrested for
homicide had previous arrests with a mean of 9.7 arrests.[18] In even
simpler terms — bad people do bad things.

John Lott's monumental study of gun ownership in the United
States covered all 3,054 U.S. counties from 1977 to 1992, supplemented with data for 1993 and 1994. He reached the following conclusion, "Of all the methods studied so far by economists, the

---

[16] David Kopel, *National Review* April 17, 2000, *An Army of Gun Lies*.
[17] Lott, *More Guns, Less Crime*, p. 8.
[18] Quoted by Wayne LaPierre in *Guns, Freedom, and Terrorism*, p. 75.

carrying of concealed handguns appears to be the most cost-effective method for reducing crime."[19] The positive effect of reducing violent crime is particularly significant for women who carry guns. Gary Kleck and David Bordua reported on an Orlando Police Department program training women in firearms safety during the late 1960s as an anti-rape measure. In the year following the well-publicized effort, there was a dramatic **88 percent decrease** in rape cases. This, despite the fact that rape statewide in Florida had increased 5 percent and nationwide by 7 percent.[20]

Incidentally, misuse of firearms by the millions of U.S. carry permit holders has proven to be virtually nil. It appears that hoplophobic[21] journalists may be more susceptible to road rage fantasies than real gun owners.

3. "Guns Are Dangerous to their Owners" Lie

Professor Lott quotes surveys that indicate that 98% of the time people use guns defensively, they merely need to brandish them before a criminal to stop the inevitable attack. According to Lott, 15 national-al polls, including those conducted by *The Los Angeles Times* and Gallup, record between 760,000 and 3.5 million defensive uses of guns per year. Florida State University Department of Criminology Professor Gary Kleck conducted a survey in 1993 which found that 2.5 million crimes are thwarted each year by gun owning Americans. His National Self-Defense Survey excluded cases where people picked up a gun to investigate suspicious noises and the like, and

---

[19] Lott, *More Guns, Less Crime*, p. 20.

[20] The 1983 study published in the *Law & Public Quarterly* is quoted *in Guns, Terrorism, and Freedom*, Wayne LaPierre, pp. 50–51.

[21] "I coined the term *hoplophobia* ... in the sincere belief that we should recognize a very peculiar sociological attitude for what it is — a more or less hysterical neurosis rather than a legitimate political position. It follows convention in the use of Greek roots in describing specific mental afflictions. *Hoplon* is the Greek word for 'instrument,' but refers synonymously to 'weapon' since the earliest and principal instruments were weapons. *Phobos* is Greek for 'terror' and medically denotes unreasoning panic rather than normal fear. Thus *hoplophobia* is a mental disturbance characterized by irrational aversion to weapons, as opposed to justified apprehension about those who may wield them." *To Ride, Shoot Straight, and Speak the Truth*, Jeff Cooper, Paladin Press, Boulder, 1988, p. 16.

focused on actual confrontations between the intended victim and the offender.[22]

Continuing further with this line of thought: one can only imagine what might have happened on September 11 had the pilots or passengers on the four hijacked airplanes been armed with handguns. My guess is they would have stopped the boxcutter-wielding terrorists. Guns would certainly have been "less dangerous" than utility knives were that day. Gun control enthusiasts (guns-in-the-hands-of-government-only) may prefer that Air Force jet fighters be used to shoot down hijacked passenger aircraft in the future. I personally see no reason why specially licensed and trained, volunteer civilian sky marshals, who agreed to carry frangible ammunition, and not consume alcohol in flight (embodying the concept of the "well regulated Militia"), be given a reasonable opportunity to defend ourselves first, before the Air Force is called in to blow us out of the sky.

4. The "Success of the Brady Law" Lie

The Clinton/Gore administration boast that half a million people were stopped by Brady Law background checks creates an interesting case of cognitive dissonance. Like those amazing body counts reported by the press during the Vietnam War that if added together would have accounted for the population of India, there seems an inherent mathematical flaw. If half a million people committed the felony of illegally attempting to purchase a weapon when they were already legally banned from such actions by Federal law, why were there less than a dozen arrests in the first seventeen months after the law was passed?[23]

5. The "Gun Show Loophole" Lie

The dreaded Gun Show loophole fretted over by the media and civilian disarmament proponents is a complete sham. If a person is engaged in gun dealing for profitable purposes, he needs to have a Federal Firearms License to do so, or he is committing a felony. If an

---

[22] Wayne La Pierre, *Guns, Crime and Freedom*, Regnery Publishing, 1994., p. 23.

[23] According to the statistics quoted by Wayne LaPierre in the April, 2000 issue of *American Rifleman*, the official publication of the NRA.

FFL dealer sells a firearm at a gun show, the exact same laws apply as if he sold it out of his store. In other words, identification must be provided by the buyer; ATF Form 4473 is filled out with the name and address of the buyer, the make, model, and serial number of the weapon, plus a series of questions regarding the buyer's legal status and mental health; a background check must be performed; and a detailed formal record of the transaction must be kept by the dealer.

QUESTION: Then what is the famous "Gun Show Loophole?"
ANSWER: Private sales that take place at Gun Shows.

In other words, as a gun owner one might want to trade up to a new rifle. Knowing a gun show was to be in town, he or she might put a little flag in the barrel of the rifle with a "For Sale" sign written on it. He would have the gun checked by the police at the door, a trigger lock put on it, and hopefully find some other person looking for a bargain. After examining and recording each other's driver's licenses to verify that it was an in-state sale, and therefore not in violation of the 1968 Gun Control Act, and asking the buyer if he is a felon (and determining to the best of one's ability that he is not), and therefore not subjecting yourself to a 10 year prison sentence for selling to a felon, fugitive or drug user, one would conclude the transaction. Alternately, if a man who had a gun collection died, and his wife needed to raise some money, she might take the collection to a gun show, rent a table, and try to sell the guns for a decent price. If she was earning a living from this, she would be a felon. However if she was truly making private sales, it would be legal in most states.

What the civilian disarmament lobby wants to do is make sure every gun is registered, and every transfer is recorded. That way, when they achieve the power to round up guns in private hands, they'll have everyone's address and know exactly what everyone owns. One of their key sophistries is that since cars are registered, why not register guns? However, unlike cars, boats, or airplanes, the possession of firearms is specifically enumerated as a right *of the people*, a right protected *from infringement* by the same Government that registers cars, boats, or airplanes. How would you feel if you had to register your books to exercise your first amendment rights?

After the September 11 attacks, gun control addicts predictably dressed their attacks on the Second Amendment in new clothing. Their faithful lapdogs in the media parroted the claim that al-Qaeda was arming itself with shotguns bought at U.S. gun shows! In January 2002, a more likely source of terrorist arms was seized by Israelis who intercepted a shipment of 50 tons of Iranian weapons being smuggled to the PLO. If anyone remembers hysterics about .50 caliber U.S. made rifles that "wound up in the hands of al-Qaeda," it might be useful to learn that those rifles were purchased directly from the manufacturer by the CIA during the 1980s, and turned over by the U.S. government to our *mujahideen* allies in Afghanistan. With prices ranging from $3,100 to $7,300, and weights from 21 pounds to 28 pounds, I wouldn't expect to see many on your local street corner anytime soon.

6. The "Other Countries Have Better Gun Laws" Lie

Other English-speaking countries have not improved their societies as much as the major news organizations would like us to believe. Dr. Miquel Faria Jr. informs us that the Australian crime rate is increasing exponentially following their 1996 gun ban. In 1998 (the first year after implementation of the ban) the Australian crime rate experienced a 44 percent increase in armed robberies, an 8.6 percent increase in aggravated assault, and a 3.2 percent increase in homicides. In the state of Victoria, there was a **three hundred percent increase** in the number of homicides committed with a firearm. In South Australia, robberies increased by nearly 60 percent. In 1999, armed robberies in Australia were up 73 percent, unarmed robberies increased by 28 percent, kidnappings 38 percent, assaults 17 percent, and manslaughter 29 percent. During the previous 25 years before banning firearms, Australia had enjoyed a steady decrease in the rate of both homicides with firearms and armed robbery.[24] Undeterred by reality, Australian gun control leader Rebecca Peters is now living in New York City, and working for an international gun-control group, funded by George Soros, that is lobbying to ban guns in civilian hands through the UN.

England has done no better. The UN Interregional Crime and Justice Institute reported in July, 2002, that Australia, England, and Wales led the seventeen nations of the industrialized Western world

[24] Miquel Faria Jr., M.D., Editor in Chief of *The Medical Sentinel*, the official publication of the Association of American Physicians and Surgeons, *Australia Crime Rate: Chaos Down Under*, published in *The New American*, May 22, 2000.

in violent crime.[25] Scholar Joyce Lee Malcolm writes of the effects of England's nearly complete ban of firearms in 1997.

> In fact a clear demonstration of the futility of gun bans, English armed crime rose 10 percent in 1998, the year after the ban on handguns. Home Office figures for April 1999 through March 2000 showed that violent crime increased 16 percent, street robberies by 26 percent — the highest ever — muggings by 28 percent, and robberies in London by nearly 40 percent. Although the overall crime rate fell slightly from 1996 to 2000, *violent crime more than doubled*. Even before these latest rises, the overall crime rate in England was 60 percent more than that in America. [emphasis added][26]

The London Sunday Times for January 16, 2000 estimated upward of 3 million illegal guns circulating in Britain. In some areas, the *Times* estimated that as many of one-third of criminals from ages 15 to 25 owned or have access to firearms.[27] In Canada and Britain, like some chilling recreation of *A Clockwork Orange*, almost half of all burglaries take place when the occupants are at home. In the well-armed United States, only 13% of burglaries are perpetrated by those brave or foolish enough to take such a risk.[28]

GUNS AND RACE

America's first state and local gun laws were nearly all designed to keep guns out of the hands of slaves. These included laws passed prior to the American Revolution. After the Civil War, nearly every American gun law sought to keep guns out of the hands of freed former slaves. Thus gun control has always had a particularly odious racial cast.

However this is also true to an alarming degree of crime. The Welfare State has failed miserably. In four decades, it has created a

---

[25] Available from http://www.unicri.it/icvs/publications/index_pub.htm, quoted in *Guns, Freedom, and Terrorism*, p. 149.
[26] *Guns and Violence: The English Experience*, Joyce Lee Malcolm, Harvard University Press, Cambridge, MA, 2002, p. 212.
[27] Robert W. Lee, *English Crime Rate*, *The New American*, April 24, 2000.
[28] Lott, *More Guns, Less Crime*, p. 5.

permanent crime-ridden underclass whose family structure has been destroyed by regulations that encourage out of wedlock births; and social and political policies that 1) pay people not to work, and 2) export manufacturing jobs overseas. Thus America has created an alternate inner city sub-culture that serves as both a permanent threat to social well-being, and an object lesson in collectivism.

Yet it also serves to provide statistics for the civilian disarmament movement. The horrific crime rate among inner city poor allows for the assertion that guns kill people who simply cannot be trusted to own a 20 ounce mechanical device; that somehow, these objects seem to exert a mysterious force — especially on the psyche of America's racial minorities. This is the justification behind the crippling spate of lawsuits filed against the gun industry in the last several years by big city mayors and the Clinton administration's Department of Housing and Urban Development. Rather than leading a chorus of outrage against this insidious racial insult, the left-wing NAACP mounted its own lawsuit against the gun industry, because of the "disproportionate" effect of gun violence in the black community.

On the other hand, there is an appalling amount of black crime. According to Department of Justice figures compiled for 1997, the incidence of black crime is proportionately far greater than white. And, a reasonable similarity appears to exist between crime figures and arrest figures. For example, according to the DOJ survey for 1997, 60 percent of robberies were reported to have been committed by blacks, while 57% of those arrested for robberies were black.[29] The FBI Uniform Crime Report for 1992 found that 55% of those arrested for murder were black, while 43.4% of murder victims were also black. The FBI report found that 94% of black victims were slain by black assailants.[30] Thus, when gun control advocates talk of banning "cheap handguns," the result of their efforts, if successful, will be to leave poor black people in high crime areas defenseless. Ironically, modern efforts at gun control are as unconscionably racist as earlier gun control policies.[31]

[29] Jared Taylor, *What Color is Crime, The Resister* Vol. 5, No. 3 Summer/Autumn 1999.
[30] John Bolton, *Counter-Propaganda 101, The Resister* Vol. 4, No, 2 Winter 1998.
[31] Conversely, the DOJ figures for interracial crime in 1994 (the most recent year in which racial statistics were gathered) report that 89% of single offender crimes and 94% of multiple offender crimes were committed by blacks against whites. If

As a law-abiding American citizen who lives in a normal environment, I refuse to be treated like some 17-year-old, out of control, inner-city gang-banger, hopped up on crack, and suffering from a dearth of moral values. My children and I were raised to exhibit both the respect for life and personal self-control that are required to enjoy the freedom to keep and bear arms.

ALARMING PRECEDENTS FOR NATIONAL GUN REGISTRATION

From 1789 to 1934 there was not one federal gun law (unless one counts the Second Amendment). The first unconstitutional gun law was passed as the 1934 National Firearms Act which sought to ban automatic weapons and silencers by burdening them with heavy taxes and unprecedented registration requirements. The next was the 1968 Gun Control Act, modeled nearly word for word on gun laws enacted by the Nazi regime

In *Gun Control: Gateway to Tyranny*, Jay Simpkin and Aaron Zelman lay out the 1938 Nazi Weapons Law with a paragraph by paragraph comparison to the U.S. Gun Control Act of 1968.[32] Anyone interested in seeking to understand the basis for U.S. gun control legislation is urged to study this fearless book. The authors also present documentary evidence that Senator Thomas Dodd (D-CT), one of the authors of the 1968 law, had several months earlier submitted official requests to the Library of Congress for an English translation of the 1938 Nazi Weapons Law.

The Nazis inherited the German 1928 Law on Firearms and Ammunition which required registration and renewable permits for firearm owners and their firearms, mandated permits for the acquisitions of ammunition, and the issuance of hunting permits. All firearms had to be stamped with serial numbers and the names of their manufacturers. When the Nazis came to power in 1933, they

---

these figures are rendered as violent crime per 100,000, 3,494 blacks out of 100,000 committed a violent crime against a white person in 1994, while 64 whites out of a 100,000 committed a violent crime against a black person. Jared Taylor, *What Color is Crime, The Resister* Vol. 5, No. 3 Summer/Autumn 1999.

[32] *Gun Control: Gateway to Tyranny*, Jay Simpkin and Aaron Zelman, Jews For the Preservation of Firearm Ownership, 1993.

thus had access to the name and home address of every legal gun owner in Germany, along with a description of his weapons.

The Nazi Weapons Law of 1938 guaranteed that only friends of the Nazi Party were able to own and carry firearms. Jews, of course, were forbidden to own guns or to participate in any business dealing in weapons. Carry permits were required in order to bear arms and were only issued to "persons of undoubted reliability, and only if a demonstration of need is set forth."[33]

Australia, Canada, and England have all recently suffered the similar fate of mandatory weapons registration followed by confiscation. Closer to home, New York City, under Mayor Lindsay, licensed rifle owners and registered their weapons in 1967, promising it would never lead to confiscation. One million rifle owners dutifully complied. In 1991, Mayor Dinkins declared so-called "assault weapons" illegal. He had only to check over two decades of registration data to confirm the names and addresses of the owners of the tens of thousands of newly-banned weapons. In 1989, California passed a law to register all "assault weapons" in that state. In 1999, another law banned all sales, transfers, and purchases of those weapons. It also declared a whole host of new weapons were now to be covered by the earlier ban. It set December 31, 1999 as the last day such a weapon could be purchased, and set December 31, 2000 as the last day such a weapon could be registered. I wonder what odds a Las Vegas bookmaker would give that one day, someone won't "pull a Dinkins" in California?

Gun Control Works to Accomplish the Wrong Results

Gun Control is a successful mechanism for the establishment of tyranny. Instituting the type of gun laws sought after by the civilian disarmament lobby would inevitably lead to a destruction of the very freedoms most Americans cherish. It is estimated that between 75 to 86 million Americans own between 200 and 240 million guns.[34] How would a government be able to check that each one of these guns is properly registered by each one of these gun owners? Who is

---

[33] Ibid, p. 59.
[34] Lott, *More Guns, Less Crime*, p.1.

going to come into *your* house to insure that a gun lock is properly installed on your weapon? Should your neighbors be encouraged to inspect your home to determine how you store your gun before allowing their children to play with yours? Should your kids be programmed to report your guns to the D.A.R.E.[35] officer in their schools? Given the nature of people, if all guns mysteriously disappeared into thin air, would the rates of murder, assault and suicide really decline?

POP QUIZ: Was the War on Drugs more effective in:
a) limiting the manufacture, availability, and use of drugs,
b) filling our nations prisons while extending the powers of the Total State?

My advice to any reader who still values freedom, and continues to assert the sacred right of self-preservation, is to make the effort to familiarize yourself with guns. Take the time and training required to learn to use a gun well. Decide that for you "gun control" means using a two-handed grip. Once you are comfortable enough to make an educated choice, buy a good one and practice with it. Join the NRA immediately and contribute regularly. Speak to your friends, family and neighbors. Make phone calls and send letters to politicians. Remind them that you intend to hold them to their oaths to defend the Constitution. Remember that no matter how many people tell you otherwise, it is still the law of the land. Consider the next time you hear some media sycophant drooling about the "international community" that our freedoms are uniquely protected by the U.S. Constitution. Each one of us had better be an active advocate of Liberty — otherwise, Liberty will vanish.

In *Naked Lunch*, William S. Burroughs describes the book's title as "a frozen moment when everyone sees what is on the end of every fork." I therefore make the following recommendation to anyone who plans to vote for any politician who endorses gun control. First, burn a copy of the Bill of Rights. Then pull the lever to cast your vote. That way, at least, you can say you had the courage to acknowledge the future you were creating.

---

[35] Drug Abuse Resistance Education, a nationwide program, founded in 1983, reaching approximately 80% of public schools, in which local police officers discuss the dangers of drug use with school children. It's motto recently morphed from "D.A.R.E. to Resist Drugs," to "D.A.R.E. to Resist Drugs and Violence."

GODDESSES, GUNS AND GUTS

Freedom is a need of the soul, and nothing else. It is in striving
toward God, that the soul strives continually after a condition of
freedom. God alone is the inciter and guarantor of freedom. . . .
Political freedom, as the Western world has known it, is only a
political reading of the Bible.
— Whittaker Chambers, *Witness*

Soon after the success of the Cuban revolution in 1959, a group of
soldiers entered the classroom. They spread themselves out,
machine guns hung from their shoulders. Their leader addressed the
assembled seven and eight-year-olds. "Children, we want you to
understand something about the revolution. Lay your heads on your
desks and close your eyes. Make a prayer to God that when you open
your eyes, you will have a container of ice cream sitting in front of
you." A long pause followed as the children prayed in the hot room.
"Now, open your eyes. — There is no ice cream. That is the value of
praying to God." Another pause. "This time, close your eyes, lay your
heads on your desks and pray to Fidel for the ice cream." The adult
who told me this story had been a little cagier than most of his class-
mates. He peeked out from between his folded arms and watched the
soldiers swiftly placing containers of ice cream on each child's desk.
The leader commanded the children in an enthusiastic tone, "Now,
open your eyes." The children were, of course, delighted.

As I write, a courageous judge in Alabama has failed to prevent
the removal of a monument, on which the Ten Commandments are
inscribed, from in front of his courthouse. The ACLU, Southern
Poverty Law Center, and other militant atheist lobby groups, fresh
from their presumptive victory in removing "under God" from the
Pledge of Allegiance, arrayed against him and the Ten Commandments in full battle dress. "[I]ts view of God, its knowledge of God, its
experience of God, is what alone gives character to a society or a
nation, and meaning to its destiny. . . . There has never been a society or a nation without God. But history is cluttered with the wreck-
age of nations that became indifferent to God, and died."[1]

[1] *Witness*, Whittaker Chambers, Random House, NY, 1952, pp. 16–17.

George Mason's 1776 Virginia Declaration of Rights was a primary influence on Thomas Jefferson's opening paragraphs of the Declaration of Independence. Mason's refusal to sign the Constitution forced those who supported its ratification to promise to add the Bill of Rights, also based on the Virginia Declaration, to encourage others to vote in their favor. The First Amendment, states in part, "Congress shall make no law respecting an establishment of religion, or prohibiting the free exercise thereof ... "

It is noteworthy that the misconstrued language of the First Amendment has become the weapon of choice of the atheist lobby to prevent people from freely exercising their religions. Like furtive smokers in New York City, those addicted to the vice of religion must confine their practice to the isolation of churches and homes, lest they contaminate a secular society with second-hand faith. Mason would have been amazed. Consider what he wrote in the last section of the Virginia Declaration of Rights.

> SECTION 16. That religion, or the duty which we owe to our Creator, and the manner of discharging it, can be directed only by reason and conviction, not by force or violence; and therefore all men are equally entitled to the free exercise of religion, according to the dictates of conscience; and that it is the mutual duty of all to practice Christian forbearance, love, and charity toward each other.[2]

Commenting on the language and context of the First Amendment (what is called "original intent"), journalist and author David Limbaugh writes, "The Establishment Clause of the First Amendment prohibits Congress from establishing a national church. It also prohibits Congress from interfering with the right of individual states to establish their own churches if they choose (between seven and nine colonies had established churches at the time of the founding) — not that any would consider it today."[3]

---

[2] US National Archives & Records Administration http://www.archives.gov/exhibit_hall/charters_of_freedom/bill_of_rights/virginia_declaration_of_rights.html.
[3] David Limbaugh, "A Closer Look at Justice Moore, the Ten Commandments, and the Rule of Law." Posted August 27, 2003 at http://www.humaneventsonline.com/article.php?id=1649.

One can imagine poor old Madelyn Murray O'Hare (the original atheist campaigner against prayer in school) rolling over in her grave. Although, since she didn't believe in the soul's survival of bodily death ... well, you can see the problem.

Here is the point I would like to make, stated in the simplest and most direct language:

Without a belief in a Higher Power to whom one is directly and personally responsible, it is impossible to live as a free man or woman.[4]

One might question why someone who thinks as I do would subscribe to a belief system that states in its political program, "There is no god but man." (See *Liber Oz* reproduced on page 113). While the definition of both "god" and "man" are well beyond the scope of this essay, it is possible to understand the term "man" as applying to a being far more exalted than a semi-rational evolved ape. Modern psychology widely accepts the existence of an unconscious mind. I hold the opinion that human beings also possess what might be called a "super-conscious" mind, and therein lies the truth of the statement, "There is no god but man."

I also accept that the alternative to the ethically aware, faith-based political and social order I am supporting here, is the UN, globalist, secular society being shoved down America's throat at an increasingly breakneck pace. In this world view, the "realist" or the "expert" has concluded that most people are not capable of governing their own lives, so they — the more self-disciplined leaders — must fill the vacuum by providing adequate controls on their moral, spiritual, and intellectual inferiors.

The human race requires discipline for its survival. At the most basic and personal level, without the discipline provided by our bone structure, we would collapse into shapeless blobs. On a more complex level, without the right ordering of human desires, society will collapse into a morass of anarchy and violence so often observed in times of crisis.

---

[4] If the Younger Brethren will unclench their fists and revive from their swoons long enough to remember the concept of aspiration to the HGA, all will be well. Those secularists who honestly believe they live up to the standards discussed on page 102 may substitute "Moral Code."

Political systems are necessarily based on discipline. Laws and social customs reward desirable behavior and punish undesirable behavior. This is far from prudery or school-marmism. It is evolution. Think of the areas of life in which people face the most danger. The military and the medical professions both come to mind. They are two of the most hierarchically observant groups in society, utilizing the most stylized and ritualistically prescribed and proscribed rules of behavior. These behavioral boundaries constitute a successful adaptation to the needs of their environments.

Anyone who has raised children is only too familiar with the consequences of behavior based solely on unbridled human desires. How many children have died or been injured by drowning, being hit by a car, or by electrocution, when indulging their own unchallenged instincts? Parents are also well-positioned to observe the natural, biological self-centered point of view of the normal child. The human socialization process involves, at its core level, the learning of proper regard for the rights of others. This culturally transmitted instruction is no less holy or unnatural because it involves tutelage. The passing on and assimilation of knowledge and codes of behavior is fully compatible with the natural dignity of our species.

Tyranny is merely a form of discipline designed to bring about the right ordering of society — in this case by external compulsion. It is not illogical in the least. The collectivist Plato even considered it the greatest good in The Republic. Caroll Quigley, mentioned in an earlier essay, was more straightforward than most, but I don't necessarily consider him an "evil" man. I think that he and many of the New World Order crowd think they are doing the right thing by attempting to manage society. After all, look at the mess we're in.[6]

In a political system that seeks to maximize individual Liberty, there must still be enough discipline to meet the needs of human survival. In the case of a free society, the requisite discipline will be self-discipline.

---

[6] However, the most egregious dishonesty of which they are guilty is not publicly accepting their own responsibility for much of that mess. Without belaboring the issue, almost every policy advanced by the U.S. Government in the last sixty years has been either created, supported, and/or administered by a member of the Council on Foreign Relations (CFR). Alger Hiss, briefly discussed in my introduction to the UN materials in appendix 2, was a member, as were Presidents Dwight Eisenhower, John Kennedy, Richard Nixon, Gerald Ford, Jimmy Carter, George H. W. Bush, and Bill Clinton.

Self discipline involves many different facets, not the least of which is learning and acting upon the lessons of the past, delaying gratification through rationally reviewing the results of behavior, and analyzing the legitimacy of a contemplated action. At the lowest level, satisfying hunger by scooping out food from a hot receptacle is behavior soon superceded by waiting for the right moment and using the appropriate instrument. On a more complex level, the sexual instinct is usually most enjoyable when unaccompanied by an unwanted pregnancy. Going further up the chain, dishonorable behavior, often extremely tempting, will lead to self-recrimination in any person with a well-developed conscience.[7]

But what is a moral standard? In my case, I base my most successful actions on what I believe is right. What I mean by "right," is that behavior by which I am prepared to be judged by a higher standard. I can call that higher standard God, and imagine It to be a white-bearded classical figure, or imagine a Hall of Judgment with the 42 Assessors awaiting Tahuti's proclamation of the results of the Weighing of my Heart against the Feather of Maat. I can calculate the effect of my behavior on the precious relationship with That which I have learned to call my Holy Guardian Angel. But whatever symbol set I might use to represent the Divine, you can bet your next paycheck it will include a sense of Fear. Holy Awe is another term to connote the same sense. It is an awareness that all I am, or can be, is secondary to a Magnificence which I cannot begin to describe, and on which I am wholly dependent. Was it not King Solomon who said Fear of the Lord is the beginning of Wisdom?

57. Follow out these my words
58. Fear nothing.
Fear nothing.
Fear nothing.
59. For I am nothing, and me thou shalt fear.[8]

---

[7] Defining "honor" is not an easy task. "Elevation of character, noblesness of mind, scorn of meanness" are all suggested by *The Oxford English Dictionary*. "Conscious self control in service to an ideal that embodies one's highest aspirations" may begin to approach the meaning.

[8] Liber LXVI, *The Holy Books of Thelema*, Equinox III, No. 9, Samuel Weiser, York Beach, ME, 1983, pp. 90–91.

I can be trusted, within the limits of my own spiritual development, to be honest, truthful, law-abiding, dependable, responsible, tolerant, care-giving, loyal, respectful, generous, etc. Part of the reason for this is my belief that my actions are being recorded by a Power to whom I am ultimately answerable. However I am equally capable of being an irresponsible, dishonest, low-life, whose selfishness and callousness is matched only by an internal compulsion to dominate every situation with which I am faced.

It's the "one from column A, one from column B" dichotomy that every self-aware human being will acknowledge — if he or she has the courage to look into the mirror of the soul. "My adepts stand upright; their head above the heavens, their feet below the hells."[9]

There is a distinct advantage to choosing for one's method of discipline a self-imposed moral code dependent on a growing understanding of a higher Power, and one's personal mission in life or True Will. The reward is a self-monitored and evolving rule of behavior, rather than one enforced by a confused 19-year-old wielding a machine gun, in subservience to leaders neither he nor I have ever met, following orders with which one or both of us may disagree. The deaths of David Koresh and 81 other members of his church, after all, rested first on the unproved assumption by a Treasury Department functionary that Koresh may have violated the $200 tax mandated for the legal conversion of semi-automatic weapons to fully automatic status.

Some further comments on this matter of respect for Authority. In the last decade, America has witnessed two very different styles of political administrations in Washington D.C., at least on the surface. The country is virtually evenly divided between those who supported Clinton and those who support Bush (assuming one supports either). What seems different from any time I remember is the visceral hatred many people feel for one or the other. The media calls this "polarization of the electorate."

But even if I happened to "like" Clinton or Bush, I would have to recognize that each of them is an imperfect being like myself. All of us are having enough trouble running our own lives. We should all exercise the courtesy and humility to stay out of each other's way. This was once called "acting like a gentleman," or "minding one's

[9] Liber XC, *The Holy Books of Thelema*, Weiser Publishing, York Beach, ME, 1983, p. 97.

own business." Neither one of these politicians, or for that matter anyone else in the world, has the right to tell me what to do.

On the other hand, I might want to do something that contradicted my own conscience or sense of morality. I may be so sorely tempted that I feel a real sense of annoyance and rebellion at realizing that what I may want is the wrong thing to do. Whether I do it or not will be based on my progress on the Spiritual Path. But at least one thing is clear. I have complete respect for (if imperfect obedience to) the source of Authority that oversees my behavior and defines my sense of right and wrong. There is no compromise or ambivalence here. But a human being, whether wearing a government hat or badge or any other symbol of authority, will never command that level of my allegiance.

Simply put, I am an imperfect being who recognizes the need for self-discipline, and is willing to be guided along the path of right action by a Power I recognize as my superior. The real advantage of inner freedom is that you get to serve a Power you respect.

Because, whether we like it or not, we will all serve a Power greater than ourselves. Those secularists who find the concept of serving God to be so repulsive or antiquated that it is beneath their dignity, condemn themselves to serve the power of man — whether it will be one tyrant with his blue-helmeted 19-year-olds, another with his ninja-clad, jack-booted storm troopers, or a cigar-sucking, communist megalomaniac whose machine-gun wielding soldiers will be trying to prove to us and our children that he is God.

A FURTHER NOTE

I showed this essay to a friend who describes himself as a secular humanist and an agnostic. In view of our conversations, I must add the following clarifications.

There are two types of humanist: secular and religious. The secular humanist is either an agnostic or an atheist. The religious humanist may, like Thomas Jefferson, be a Deist who believes the world was created by a God who is uninvolved in the later affairs of His creation.

There are further differences among humanists. Individualists believe the fundamental concern for humanist thought should be the well-being and sanctity of the individual. They believe a person "owns" his own mind and body, that property is inviolate, therefore one must not be forced to any action that infringes his will. (Of course, conversely, the individual must not initiate force or violence against another.) Statists or collectivists hold a contrasting viewpoint. They believe the guiding principle against which humanist thought should be weighed is the interest and well-being of the group (as defined by the government or the "experts") which supercedes any rights of the individual . Both individualists and statists believe their program will result in the "greatest good" for humanity.

Libertarian humanists (individualists) are those who focus on individual rights. Many of America's Founders could be called libertarian religious humanists. Communist and socialist humanists (statists or collectivists) follow the school of thought that runs from the disciples of Rousseau during the French Revolution, through Karl Marx, to the likes of today's Howard Dean or Hillary Clinton.

I am happy to count as a friend any person with a well-developed ethical sense who does not believe in God, if he or she is honest and self-disciplined enough to understand the difference between "enlightened self interest" and self-indulgence; and who regards the rights of the individual as the absolute basis for his humanist beliefs. One of my intellectual heroes is Ayn Rand, an atheist, whose devotion to the highest ethical standards was, I believe, unsurpassed by the religious luminaries whom I also regard with admiration and respect.

SUGGESTED ACTIONS

The only thing necessary for the triumph of evil is for good men to do nothing. — Edmund Burke

If this book has come anywhere close to its intended goal of stimulating an awareness of the value of freedom, you may be feeling a sense of disquiet. How can anyone work to reverse the trend toward tyranny? I frankly do not know if it is possible to change the course of modern life and regain our freedoms. I am quite familiar with the feeling that the dark weight of inevitability renders all resistance futile. Yet, in more courageous moments, I continue to believe that our thoughts, hopes, and aspirations live on beyond us; perhaps in a collective unconscious, cosmic human eidolon, astral plane (or higher) thought form, or maybe just in the genes of our children. I would rather die fighting for freedom than live as a slave. This is not meant to sound romantic. I resist because it is my nature to resist. If you choose to lie down and play dead in a docile gesture of acceptance: Please put this book down, raise your hands above your head, and say, "I surrender." You are now free to wave and get misty-eyed when the UN Secretary General's limousine passes you in the street.

Those of us who remain might begin by acknowledging that we are bucking a tide so enormous it seems to be swallowing the entire world. If we do nothing more than hold our individual weight against that tide, we will, if nothing else, imperceptibly alter its direction. If enough people will do only that, it will make a change. Some can do more. In time, more will be able to do more. One day, we will take back the freedoms that are our birthright. Maybe this will not occur in our own lifetimes. But the efforts we make here and now will not be wasted, despite whatever course of events we may experience.

LOOK WITHIN

Perhaps the best way to begin is to look inside ourselves as honestly as possible and ask certain questions. Take a few breaths, and quietly cast the mind's eye inward. Ask yourself how many times the government, or a law, or regulation has actually been of tangible personal benefit to you as an individual. Next question: What has government, or its laws, done to change your personal behavior? How often has the threat of a law or punishment prevented you personally from committing an act that violates either your own code of ethics, or the inalienable rights of another person?

The next step is to investigate those parts of yourself that call out for external control. If you believe that reality conforms, in part, to your thoughts and psychic needs (and I do), ask yourself this question: What *need of mine* is being met by this intrusive infringement on my personal space by swarms of busybodies and tyrants seeking to limit my choices? How have I allowed myself to be vulnerable? What inherent iniquity has so weakened my psychic integrity that I can be legally forced to fasten my seatbelt, or compelled to financially support a moronic cause I despise. Don't get too picky about words. If you prefer, change "iniquity" to "refusal or reluctance to pursue my Will."

More questions: Of what personal evasion of responsibility have I been guilty? What compromise with evil have I made? What tarnish have I left unpolished on my armor? What dullness, left unsharpened, renders my own weapons less efficient? Where is the break in my Circle that has allowed this Demon to intrude? That which lurks will consume nobility and light, and vomit back servility and darkness. How can I strengthen my spiritual life to thwart this force?

Periods of such regular introspection will allow for more efficient, practical behavior. Without it, we will be mere political activists. To triumph, we must become spiritual revolutionaries operating on a political plane. Here are some basic practical steps toward maximizing Liberty and turning away the foetid hand of state control. You will add others as your awareness matures.

EDUCATE YOURSELF

This is the first and most important part of maintaining and regaining our political freedom. *The Federalist Papers* and *The Anti-Federalist Papers* are both available in mass market paperback.[1] For about

---

[1] For full bibliographic data on the titles mentioned here, please see Recommended Reading beginning on page 217.

$13, you can read some of the most intelligent and poignant discussions in history, and hear the hopes and fears for freedom of America's Founders. If nothing else, it will give you a sense of the travesty involved the next time some drooling moron uses the expression, "rich, fat, white males" or tells you the Founding Fathers were slaveholding Christians who should be ignored. These writings are also the primary reference source for "original intent." In other words, when the Constitution and the Bill of Rights were written, what did the authors mean?

The Law by Frederick Bastiat provides an excellent philosophical framework to understand the dangers of modern day statism. Written in France in 1853, its message has stood the test of time. *Lost Rights* and *Freedom in Chains*, both by James Bovard, will give you an up-to-date catalogue of the severity of the problems we face right now. Bovard's newest book, *Terrorism and Tyranny* released in September of 2003, presents an analysis of the Patriot Act and a close look at the War on Terror. It will cause you to take a hard look at the balance between security and liberty.

Invaluable data on the history and nature of the internationalist tyranny is provided by John McManus in *Financial Terrorism*, William Jasper in *Global Tyranny*, and *The United Nations Exposed*, and James Perloff in *Shadows of Power*. These four books discuss the New World Order in frightening but sane detail. They are well-researched, and scrupulously annotated with source materials from the public record. *Global Tyranny* contains a humorous chapter on the New Age movement that displays considerable ignorance — but we can separate the wheat from the chaff, can we not? In fact, much of the criticism he raises about the New Age movement is accurate. He describes it as having been co-opted by left wing activists camouflaging their true agenda in eco-spiritual terms. Gorbachev and his ilk as the high priests of a socialist cult disguised as paganism, whose actual purpose is the Marxist goal of eliminating private property. Those who dispute this, might visit http://www.arkofhope.org.

Another interesting little volume is called *The Occult Technology of Power* by Peter McAlpine. It is an fictionalized account of the intellectual training program designed for a young prime mover behind the Internationalist Superstate. The cynical agenda of the would-be global tyrants, as posited by this book, will, in the words of a friend, "hang like a bat in your mind." *One Day in the Life of Ivan Denisovich* by Aleksandr Solzhenitsyn provides an invaluable glimpse into the reality perfectly fictionalized by George Orwell in *1984*. Add *Brave New World* by Aldous Huxley to those mentioned above, and you can claim to have an educated grasp of the problem.

Get together with intelligent friends and suggest some of these books. Form discussion groups among yourselves. Make an effort to stay on topic. You might experiment by attempting to find the Constitutional principle behind each action that appears in the news. Remember that the phrase "general welfare" in the Constitution was not originally intended as a catch-all phrase to negate each of the restrictions placed on government by the Constitution. You will find that very few programs or activities of the government today are legal according to the mandate by which our rulers rule.

INVESTIGATE DIFFERENT NEWS SOURCES

Alternative news sources will help you to understand exactly how biased the media is. CNN is not broadcasting the truth. *The New York Times* does not give us all the news fit to print. *The New American Magazine* is an excellent Constitutionally oriented news source. Though it frequently displays a Christian bias, dare to discriminate, and you will be rewarded with a rich flow of ideas unlike any you will encounter in other media. I regularly check the establishment Reuters news feed through Yahoo, the Drudge Report, WorldNet Daily, and Human Events websites for my daily news reports, and just discovered FrontPage Magazine. A new website, http://www.warengine.us offers a superb collection of recommended links for in-depth electronic sources of study of many critical issues.

SPEAK OPENLY

Become a Voice for these ideas. The late William Burroughs equated ideas to viruses. Become a carrier. When you listen to some half-wit declaim about white males, say something. When you're on the phone, make jokes about modern topics. Issues like treason are wonderful conversation pieces. If a government official receives money from an enemy, and then uses his political power to sell weapons and technology to that enemy, who then uses those weapons and that technology to target American cities with nuclear bombs — is that treason? Here's another. If Iraq has the second largest oil resources in the world, why even suggest that American tax dollars be given as a gift for Iraqi reconstruction? By what logic would it be in America's self-interest that loans made to the profligate and corrupt Hussein regime (primarily by France, Germany, and Russia) be repaid with money taken from our citizens? Are we facing a sudden shortage of bad roads, hungry people, and aging infrastructure in this country?

EXERCISE YOUR SECOND AMENDMENT RESPONSIBILITIES

Buy guns. Learn to shoot safely. Remember, the proper definition of gun control is being able to hit your target. Legal guns in the hands of law-abiding citizens are a priority, according to (white male) Noah Webster, who wrote in 1787, "Before a standing army can rule, the people must be disarmed; as they are in almost every kingdom in Europe." (Things haven't really changed that much, have they?)

Tyranny is not possible in an armed society. The more guns in the hands of law-abiding American civilians, the more difficult it will be for UN sponsored "international consensus-building efforts" to take them away. I quoted one of Kofi Annan's pleas to overturn America's Second Amendment in Pulling Liberty's Teeth. In addition to his pulpit pounding, in July 2003, the UN convened the first meeting of its absurdly named Biennial Meeting of States on the Implementation of the Program of Action on Small Arms and Light Weapons in All Its Aspects. The next meeting is scheduled for 2005 (giving them time, one imagines, to come up with a catchy acronym). The meeting's goal should come as no surprise to the attentive reader; they want to make civilian ownership of firearms illegal worldwide, thus achieving the dream of a global police state — guns in the hands of soldiers, police and designated bureaucrats.

You MUST join the National Rifle Association to fight for the Second Amendment. Gun Owners of America is also an excellent and active group. Join both, because the NRA membership is always the one that gets counted by the collectivist media. Educate yourself in the Second Amendment. Understand why Patrick Henry said, "The great object is that every man be armed." Don't take offense. Remember that if he said it today, it would read, "The great object is that every man and every woman be armed." Incidentally, he is not talking about duck hunting. As he further explains:

Guard with jealous attention the public liberty. Suspect every one who approaches that jewel. Unfortunately, nothing will preserve it but downright force. Whenever you give up that force, you are inevitably ruined.

In other words, if guns are outlawed, only governments will have guns.

PRINCIPLE: You do not ever surrender your personal weapons any-where, anytime. To do so is to place yourself in the physical pow-er of others whose intentions can never be known to you in advance.[2]

TAKE AN INTEREST

As I said earlier, simple reflection on these issues is not enough. Just look at Tibet, an exalted spiritual culture laid waste by Chinese com-munist genocidal hordes, while the rest of the "international com-munity" was too busy "engaging" China to exactly notice.

The Tyrants are silently erecting the walls of your cells and forg-ing your chains as you sit reading these words. America is the last bastion of political freedom on earth. The American system is the only one in which the natural rights of the individual are recognized as stronger than either the will of the majority, or the whim of the government. If the Constitution can survive as the Law of the Land in America we have a chance. That's why statists are working so hard to emasculate it.

GET INVOLVED

Find politicians and lobbying groups you can support and contribute to their efforts. I have primarily concerned myself with Second Amendment activism, but I also support people like Libertarian Congressman Dr. Ron Paul, who is working to pass legislation to withdraw from the UN. I don't have a lot of discretionary income,

---

[2] Jeff Cooper, C Stories, Tempe, AZ, Wisdom Publishing, 2004, p. 103.

but I have determined that regular financial support of carefully chosen Constitutional advocacy efforts is an absolutely necessary expense.

Avoid touchy-feely, self-esteem, "victim rights" causes. It doesn't matter whether you applaud or condemn a corporation for supporting or rejecting gay spousal healthcare. This is a non-issue designed to neutralize intelligent people who seek to promote freedom, but who can be manipulated into focusing their energies on lesser issues. Pay attention to real issues. If you see the letter of the Constitution or the Bill of Rights violated, go for it. The Second Amendment is not the only target of modern statists. If you want to make yourself more ill, look into the battle against the First, Fourth, Fifth and Sixth Amendments being conducted in the name of Campaign Finance reform, the War on Terror, and the War on Drugs.

Politicians are responsive to public opinion. While many Americans sit in their living rooms drooling at the command of the media, concerned people can write letters to their representatives. (Do you know the name of your Congressman?) While the folks in Congress may not be geniuses, they can count to two. And every two years they will face you at the polls. They have all kinds of formulas taught by their handlers about how many voters each personal letter actually represents. Make phone calls. Send emails. Always be polite. Remember, these folks can literally kill you if you appear to threaten them. Remind them of the Constitutional issues touching the matters of your concern. They swear an oath to uphold and defend the Constitution. Remind them of that oath. Be polite. Be persistent. Pretend that you are a Secret Service agent reading your letter. Is the writer a concerned citizen, or a dangerous nut? Be polite. Be persistent.

Write letters to newspapers. If you speak and write well enough, maybe they'll publish it, and give you the opportunity to reach others. Maybe just one employee in a newspaper office will realize in a flash that one mind has refused to consume its force-fed ration. Write to TV networks. Complain to the FCC if you find political bias. Call in to radio talk shows. Make your ideas heard. Do your research. Write a book like this. If it's good enough, I'll buy it. I promise.

Be creative. Maybe you are qualified to start an alternative school for kids, one that will avoid the indoctrination efforts of the left wing public school system suffered through by most American children. Not only will your kids be able to read, add, and subtract, they just might be encouraged to learn how to think. There are many freedom-centered activities out there. The possibilities are limited only by our imaginations. But they all require careful thought and sustained action.

Use Common Sense

Ask yourself some hard questions about the viability of the assumptions that are taken for granted in the "intellectual" gestalt, or "public discourse," of modern America. Test these ideas for yourself by examining them under the microscopic scrutiny of your most determined ability to reason. Can they possibly be true? If you decide they are not, the next question to ask is whether the people who feed them into the national psyche are stupid or sinister? You needn't answer yet. It takes time to tear off that particular veil.

ON IMMIGRATION. If American compassion and prosperity have produced a tax supported social safety net for citizens in danger, can it survive the unchecked swarms of sick and impoverished *illegal* immigrants, who are entitled by our laws to receive free medical care, welfare benefits, and bilingual education the minute they sneak across the border? Do you believe socialists may have a hidden agenda served by enfranchising immigrants who will ever demand more services from the welfare state? Here's another question: Are today's illegal immigrants — surreptitiously slipping across a border in defiance of the laws of America, in search of seasonal work, with their political and cultural loyalty firmly attached to their country of birth — really in the same category as the early twentieth century immigrant who came to the U.S. legally, took the oath of citizenship, was inspected for infectious diseases, and was anxious to become an American citizen in every sense of the word? (My mother didn't speak English until she entered school at age 5. Then she taught English to her parents.)

ON "VOTING RIGHTS." Most of us remember the butterfly ballot and hanging chads of the 2000 presidential election. Let's think for a moment about voting rights and common sense. The butterfly ballot was designed by a Democratic party official to make it easier for the elderly to vote. Perhaps it was a flawed design. My question is this:

Can someone, who does not have the rational faculties to figure out the layout of the butterfly ballot, have the competence to decide on who should control the largest nuclear arsenal on the face of the planet? Same question for someone who doesn't understand he must stick a pin all the way through a piece of index card stock in order for his vote to be counted by a machine. How about this: Should people receiving public assistance have the right to periodically vote themselves a raise from the assets of taxpaying voters? Or this: Can someone who does not speak English, and/or is unable to read, have the ability to form a coherent understanding of the serious issues involved in an American election?

On internationalism. In 1953, during the height of the Cold War, a Congressional investigator named Norman Dodd was invited to visit the Ford Foundation in the course of a study of the policies of tax exempt public foundations. H. Rowan Gaither, a CFR member and president of the institution, told the astonished young man that the substance of White House directives guiding the Ford Foundation was to use its grant-making powers, "so to alter life in the United States that we can be comfortably merged with the Soviet Union." My question here is this: Given that Americans have more individual political liberties than citizens of any nation on earth, do you believe that globalists intend to raise the level of the political rights of people in other countries, or do you believe they intend to lessen the rights of American citizens? I would ask the same question for the multi-thousand page "free trade" agreements both Republican and Democrat presidents sign with such regularity in recent years. Do the financial interests that sponsor these agreements intend to raise the standard of living of people in the rest of the world to equal those of Americans, or do you think they intend to lower the standard of living of Americans?

On capitalism. Keeping in mind Robert Heinlein's doctrine of *Tanstaafl* ("There ain't no such thing as a free lunch") described in *The Moon Is a Harsh Mistress*, ask yourself this: Who is going to pay for all the social programs everyone seems to want? Again: If American tax rates skyrocket to equal those of the socialist countries in Europe, is it not probable that our economy will become as anemic as their own?

American drug companies have become the latest piñata in the ongoing campaign against capitalism. Any reader with a friend or loved one over 40 probably knows someone whose life has been saved or maintained by the use of expensive drugs. Many of these loved ones may have first tried "holistic" or herbal cures that were ineffective. While I am a great believer in natural healing for most medical conditions, I have personal experience with the limitations of alternative medicine. I am also aware, because of my research on the Crusades, that the average life expectancy for a medieval European was 35 years when herbs were the sole available medical technology. My question is this: Did the life-saving drugs that have worked for so many people in the modern world originate in the laboratories of Europe, where government price controls deter scientists from developing new drugs?

ON "AFFIRMATIVE ACTION." Can intelligent white children maintain their ambition to excel if they are denied entrance to higher education, or jobs, based on the color of their skin. Is reverse discrimination *fair*? Can the sins of discrimination be atoned for by the sins of discrimination?

ON HYPHENATED-AMERICANISM. Will society ever be able to recover from the balkanization imposed by modern politically correct language conventions, mandating the use of terms such as "African-American," "Hispanic-American," "Arab-American," "Japanese-American," etc.? Keeping in mind the linguistic requirements of both traditional chivalry and modern feminism, if a child is born from the union of a Hispanic father and an Arab mother, is the child an Arab-Hispanic-American, or a Hispanic-Arab-American? Are there any "Americans" left in America? If so, who would they be?

AND FINALLY. Does the Supreme Court really need to legislate sexual behavior so we can have more fun in bed?

Liber LXXVII

Oz:

"the law of
the strong:
this is our law
and the joy
of the world."
— *AL. II. 21.*

"Do what thou wilt shall be the whole of the Law."
— *AL. I. 40.*

"thou has no right but to do thy will. Do that, and no
other shall say nay." — *AL. I. 42–3.*

"Every man and every woman is a star." — *AL. I. 3.*

There is no god but man.

1. Man has the right to live by his own law —
    to live in the way that he wills to do:
    to work as he will:
    to play as he will:
    to rest as he will:
    to die when and how he will.

2. Man has the right to eat what he will:
    to drink what he will:
    to dwell where he wills to dwell:
    to move as he will on the face of the earth.

3. Man has the right to think what he will:
    to speak what he will:
    to write what he will:
    to draw, paint, carve, etch, mould, build as he will:
    to dress as he will.

4. Man has the right to love as he will: —
    "take your fill and will of love as ye will,
    when, where and with whom ye will." — *AL. I. 51.*

5. Man has the right to kill those who would thwart
    these rights.

    "the slaves shall serve." — *AL. II. 58.*

    "Love is the law, love under will." — *AL. I. 57.*

Aleister Crowley

ALEISTER CROWLEY ON
LIBER OZ AND AMERICAN LIBERTY

By the way, about attracting people to the O.T.O., I still think *Liber Oz* is the best bet. There is a vile threat to the "rugged American individualism" that actually *created* the U.S.A. by the bureaucratic crowd who want society to be a convict prison.

"Safety first" — there is no "social insecurity," no fear for the future, no anxiety about what to do next — in Sing Sing.

All the totalitarian schemes add up to the same in the end. And the approach is so insidious, the arguments so subtle and irrefutable, the advantages so obvious — that the danger is very real, very imminent, very difficult to bring home to the average citizen, who sees only the immediate gain, and is hoodwinked as to the price that must be paid for it.

Liber Oz was published by Aleister Crowley in 1941. It was designed to be an unequivocal statement of the rights of man written in words of one syllable. The text above on the relation between *Liber Oz* and American liberty is extracted from a letter written by Crowley to Karl Germer, his representative in America, and, upon Crowley's death in 1947, his successor as Outer Head of the O.T.O. or Ordo Templi Orientis. (Letter in Yorke collection at the Warburg Institute, London, dated March 8 [no year, but probably 1945]. Reproduced by kind permission of Ordo Templi Orientis.)

APPENDIX ONE

The Language of Freedom

"We the people of the United States, in order to form a more perfect union, establish justice, insure domestic tranquility, provide for the common defense, promote the general welfare, and secure the blessings of liberty to ourselves and our posterity, do ordain and establish this Constitution for the United States of America."

With these words, America's founders launched a unique political experiment. For the first time in history, a government was established by a group of people who were all of the following:

- Well schooled in the historical precedent of all recorded previous experiments,
- Fiercely determined to protect their Liberty, so much so in fact that they were working in the shadow of a bloody revolution fought against overwhelming odds and a far more powerful force.
- Despite their nearly miraculous victory, surrounded on all sides by enemies. Britain, against whom they had fought, was a bitter, humiliated enemy, ready at a moment's notice to avenge their defeat. France, though something of an ally during the Revolution, was, perhaps not surprisingly, no one's friend. Spain sat on the continent ready to strike from Mexico in an instant. Indian tribes, displaced by the settlers were in a state of constant hostility.
- Facing an economic crisis of major proportions due to war debts from the Revolution, and the constant turmoil of disparate tariff and tax laws among the 13 states, which made commerce and the free flow of goods difficult when not impossible.
- Working to establish 13 fiercely independent states into a union that would serve to better defend them all, but at the cost of sacrificing some of their autonomy to an untested Federal system.

Most were God-fearing men. To state that many were Deists or Masons, rather than Christians, is to belabor the issue. When they stood before the magnificence of the sky, or the sea, or the mountain, or the miracle of a child's birth, their hearts were filled with a sense of awe at the Power that brought those miracles to existence. Nor were they simply an eighteenth century phenomena. For the atheist revolution that tore France apart was fought in the name of secular goals, laced with anger, greed, and envy. As the blood soaked guillotine continued its inexorable campaign against the rich, the powerful, the dissenter, the shop-keeper against whom a grudge was held, no one dared raise the specter of morality, at least not publicly. This was in marked contrast to the revolution a decade earlier in America, where a basic respect for life generally confined the carnage to the battlefield; where retribution was minimal, more the excited passion of the moment than the evil policy of a regime of sociopaths like those who seized power in France. Against Danton and Robespierre — and later Lenin, Stalin and Mao — America holds the image of George Washington and Thomas Jefferson.

There are no platitudes in the preamble to the American Constitution quoted above. Maybe that's one reason, despite all the efforts to kill it for over two centuries, especially in the last, it survives as the oldest written legal structure still in force in any nation on earth. Compare these words to those of the UN Charter reproduced in appendix two. Maybe a dash of humility was what was needed. Where America's founders sought simply common defense, general welfare, and the assurance of liberty, the UN seeks to eliminate war (for the first time since some post-monkey grabbed a rock in anger) and to help the people of the world practice tolerance and live together as good neighbors (despite the singular failure of millennia of religious and philosophical teachings to accomplish anything of the sort). I'll make a public prediction that the UN Charter does not survive two centuries.

The first ten Amendments to the Constitution were not designed to change it. They were designed to augment it, and were part of the stock-in-trade of those who sought it's ratification. In other words, "no Bill of Rights, no agreement," was the cry of the day. See the Preamble to the Bill of Rights which follows. Personally I think we could have survived quite well by just adding the Thirteenth Amendment to those ten, and been a lot better off without most of the others, especially the sixteenth and seventeenth.

We must address that critical subject that has drained this nation of so much of its blood and moral virility, and which may yet prove our undoing — the sin of slavery. I call it a sin knowing full well that it continues to exist today in African and Arab lands, and that for millennia it was viewed as a normal consequence of military defeat, economic deprivation, or the vicissitudes of power. Slavery must rival prostitution as the oldest human institution. I do not believe an objective study of mankind's existence on this planet will find many races, nations, religious or other groups who were not, at one time or another, enslaved by a rival race, nation, religious or other group; nor who, given the opportunity, failed to enslave others. Equally true is that one will always find traitors and profiteers among the enslaved who facilitated the trade in the flesh and lives of their brothers and sisters. Slavery has been an unpleasant fact of life for most of human history.[1]

During the Constitutional Convention in 1787, Colonel George Mason of Virginia complained that the British government had prevented Virginia from ending the slave trade. In 1662 the Royal African Company had been incorporated, headed by the Duke of York, with the King of England as a large shareholder. The chief profit of this company was derived from the exportation of African slaves to the plantations of the English colonies in America. Thus slavery was a long established institution at the time of the Constitutional Convention. In the northern industrial states slavery had faded out as an inefficient means of production. But in the southern cotton and rice producing economy, it had taken a firm hold.

The desperate straits of the thirteen colonies drove them to create their union at all costs, despite the abhorrence of slavery expressed by many, and the bitter arguments about it during the Convention. George Mason prophetically observed that, "Every master of slaves is born a petty tyrant. They bring the judgment of heaven on a Country. As nations cannot be rewarded or punished in the next world they must be in this. By an inevitable chain of causes and effects, providence punishes national sins by national calamities."[2] In part because of his strong feelings against slavery, he refused to sign the Constitution.

During the Convention's debates on slavery, slave ownership in France, England, and Holland were cited as examples of modern states which condoned the practice. On the other hand, one of the last societies on earth to own slaves legally has done more in the world to eliminate slavery than any other nation or ideology in

[1] I mentioned in *The Templars and the Assassins: The Militia of Heaven*, that of the thirty-seven Abbasid caliphs, all but three were sons of slave mothers.
[2] *The Anti-Federalist Papers and the Constitutional Convention Debates*, ed. Ralph Ketcham, Mentor Books, Penquin, New York, 1986, p. 162

history. I refer of course to the Judaeo-Christian based American society which finally eliminated slavery in its own land with the Thirteenth Amendment in 1865, and has worked ceaselessly against it elsewhere in the world ever since.

To criticize America's founders for their position on slavery is ironic in this regard. In a lifetime of watching TV, reading magazines and newspapers, and discussing current events with most people I know, I must have heard about America's slave owning founders a thousand times. (Former-President Clinton even apologized for it in Africa.) However, I have almost never heard the popular press criticize liberal icon Franklin Roosevelt for his behavior at Yalta in allowing Russia three votes in the newly-forming UN, nor his handing over of millions of Eastern Europeans into Soviet slavery — though he knew at the time that Stalin was responsible for the deaths of tens of millions of his Soviet subjects. Similarly, I have almost never heard the popular media criticize U.S. State Department support for the rise of Mao-tse-Tung in China, nor express any condemnation about the estimated 35 million Chinese citizens whom Mao slaughtered while in power. This does not make slavery right. Far from it. But it does cause one to wonder about the information flow that forms popular culture.

Having initially planned to include only the Declaration of Independence and the Bill of Rights here, after some internal debate I decided to include the full text of the Constitution along with later Amendments. While it is a long and complicated text, I have no problem with this book being able to serve as a reference guide to the structure of Limited Government. Note the magnificent checks and balances contained herein, and the subtleties throughout. One of the most important lessons is how ignorant our modern electorate is on this topic. By way of illustration, we have all heard complaints about the Supreme Court, from both the left and the right of the political spectrum. A glance at Article 3, Section 2, Paragraph 2 shows how easy it can be to solve that problem if necessary.

This is a country founded by visionaries and revolutionaries designed to be run by a committed and intelligent citizenry. With effort and courage, we can keep ourselves and America free.

Let us begin with Declaration of Independence, the quintessential statement of Liberty in the world today. This elegant masterpiece came from the pen of Thomas Jefferson.

The Declaration of Independence

(Adopted in Congress July 4, 1776)

The Unanimous Declaration of
the Thirteen United States of America

When, in the course of human events, it becomes necessary for one people to dissolve the political bonds which have connected them with another, and to assume among the powers of the earth, the separate and equal station to which the laws of nature and of nature's God entitle them, a decent respect to the opinions of mankind requires that they should declare the causes which impel them to the separation.

We hold these truths to be self-evident, that all men are created equal, that they are endowed by their Creator with certain unalienable rights, that among these are life, liberty and the pursuit of happiness. That to secure these rights, governments are instituted among men, deriving their just powers form the consent of the governed. That whenever any form of government becomes destructive to these ends, it is the right of the people to alter or to abolish it, and to institute new government, laying its foundation on such principles and organizing its powers in such form, as to them shall seem most likely to effect their safety and happiness. Prudence, indeed, will dictate that governments long established should not be changed for light and transient causes; and accordingly all experience hath shown that mankind are more disposed to suffer, while evils are sufferable, than to right themselves by abolishing the forms to which they are accustomed. But when a long train of abuses and usurpations, pursuing invariably the same object evinces a design to reduce them under absolute despotism, it is their right, it is their duty, to throw off such government, and to provide new guards for their future security. — Such has been the patient sufferance of these colonies; and such is now the necessity which constrains them to alter their former systems of government. The history of the present King of Great Britain is a history of repeated injuries and usurpations, all having in direct object the establishment of an absolute tyranny over these states. To prove this, let facts be submitted to a candid world.

He has refused his assent to laws, the most wholesome and necessary for the public good.

He has forbidden his governors to pass laws of immediate and pressing importance, unless suspended in their operation till his assent should be obtained; and when so suspended, he has utterly neglected to attend to them.

He has refused to pass other laws for the accommodation of large districts of people, unless those people would relinquish the right of representation in the legislature, a right inestimable to them and formidable to tyrants only.

He has called together legislative bodies at places unusual, uncomfortable, and distant from the depository of their public records, for the sole purpose of fatiguing them into compliance with his measures.

He has dissolved representative houses repeatedly, for opposing with manly firmness his invasions on the rights of the people.

He has refused for a long time, after such dissolutions, to cause others to be elected; whereby the legislative powers, incapable of annihilation, have returned to the people at large for their exercise; the state remaining in the meantime exposed to all the dangers of invasion from without, and convulsions within.

He has endeavored to prevent the population of these states; for that purpose obstructing the laws for naturalization of foreigners; refusing to pass others to encourage their migration hither, and raising the conditions of new appropriations of lands.

He has obstructed the administration of justice, by refusing his assent to laws for establishing judiciary powers.

He has made judges dependent on his will alone, for the tenure of their offices, and the amount and payment of their salaries.

He has erected a multitude of new offices, and sent hither swarms of officers to harass our people, and eat out their substance.

He has kept among us, in times of peace, standing armies without the consent of our legislature.

He has affected to render the military independent of and superior to civil power.

He has combined with others to subject us to a jurisdiction foreign to our constitution, and unacknowledged by our laws; giving his assent to their acts of pretended legislation:

For quartering large bodies of armed troops among us:

For protecting them, by mock trial, from punishment for any

murders which they should commit on the inhabitants of these states:

For cutting off our trade with all parts of the world:

For imposing taxes on us without our consent:

For depriving us in many cases, of the benefits of trial by jury:

For transporting us beyond seas to be tried for pretended offenses:

For abolishing the free system of English laws in a neighboring province, establishing therein an arbitrary government, and enlarging its boundaries so as to render it at once an example and fit instrument for introducing the same absolute rule in these colonies:

For taking away our charters, abolishing our most valuable laws, and altering fundamentally the forms of our governments:

For suspending our own legislatures, and declaring themselves invested with power to legislate for us in all cases whatsoever.

He has abdicated government here, by declaring us out of his protection and waging war against us.

He has plundered our seas, ravaged our coasts, burned our towns, and destroyed the lives of our people.

He is at this time transporting large armies of foreign mercenaries to complete the works of death, desolation and tyranny, already begun with circumstances of cruelty and perfidy scarcely paralleled in the most barbarous ages, and totally unworthy the head of a civilized nation.

He has constrained our fellow citizens taken captive on the high seas to bear arms against their country, to become the executioners of their friends and brethren, or to fall themselves by their hands.

He has excited domestic insurrections amongst us, and has endeavored to bring on the inhabitants of our frontiers, the merciless Indian savages, whose known rule of warfare, is undistinguished destruction of all ages, sexes and conditions.

In every stage of these oppressions we have petitioned for redress in the most humble terms: our repeated petitions have been answered only by repeated injury. A prince, whose character is thus marked by every act which may define a tyrant, is unfit to be the ruler of a free people.

Nor have we been wanting in attention to our British brethren. We have warned them from time to time of attempts by their legislature to extend an unwarrantable jurisdiction over us. We have

reminded them of the circumstances of our emigration and settlement here. We have appealed to their native justice and magnanim-
ity, and we have conjured them by the ties of our common kindred
to disavow these usurpations, which, would inevitably interrupt our
connections and correspondence. We must, therefore, acquiesce in
the necessity, which denounces our separation, and hold them, as we
hold the rest of mankind, enemies in war, in peace friends.

We, therefore, the representatives of the United States of America, in General Congress, assembled, appealing to the Supreme Judge
of the world for the rectitude of our intentions, do, in the name, and
by the authority of the good people of these colonies, solemnly publish and declare, that these united colonies are, and of right ought to
be free and independent states; that they are absolved from all allegiance to the British Crown, and that all political connection
between them and the state of Great Britain, is and ought to be
totally dissolved; and that as free and independent states, they have
full power to levy war, conclude peace, contract alliances, establish
commerce, and to do all other acts and things which independent
states may of right do. And for the support of this declaration, with
a firm reliance on the protection of Divine Providence, we mutually
pledge to each other our lives, our fortunes and our sacred honor.

The Constitution of the United States

Approved by the Convention of States, September 17, 1787
Certified by the Continental Congress on September 13, 1788

(Material printed in italics is no longer in effect)

We the people of the United States, in order to form a more perfect union, establish justice, insure domestic tranquility, provide for the common defense, promote the general welfare, and secure the blessings of liberty to ourselves and our posterity, do ordain and establish this Constitution for the United States of America.

Article I

SECTION 1. All legislative powers herein granted shall be vested in a Congress of the United States, which shall consist of a Senate and House of Representatives.

SECTION 2. The House of Representatives shall be composed of members chosen every second year by the people of the several States, and the electors in each State shall have the qualifications requisite for electors of the most numerous branch of the State legislature.

No person shall be a Representative who shall not have attained to the age of twenty five years, and been seven years a citizen of the United States, and who shall not, when elected, be an inhabitant of that State in which he shall be chosen.

Representatives and direct taxes shall be apportioned among the several States which may be included within this Union, *according to their respective numbers, which shall be determined by adding to the whole number of free persons, including those bound to service for a term of years, and excluding Indians not taxed, three fifths of all other Persons.*[1] The actual Enumeration shall be made within three years after the first meeting of the Congress of the United States, and within every subsequent term of ten years, in such manner as they shall by law direct. *The number of Representatives shall not exceed one for every thir-*

---

[1] See Fourteenth Amendment.

ty thousand, but each State shall have at least one Representative; and until such enumeration shall be made, the State of New Hampshire shall be entitled to choose three, Massachusetts eight, Rhode Island and Providence Plantations one, Connecticut five, New York six, New Jersey four, Pennsylvania eight, Delaware one, Maryland six, Virginia ten, North Carolina five, South Carolina five, and Georgia three.[2]

When vacancies happen in the Representation from any State, the executive authority thereof shall issue writs of election to fill such vacancies.

The House of Representatives shall choose their speaker and other officers; and shall have the sole power of impeachment.

SECTION 3. The Senate of the United States shall be composed of two Senators from each State, *chosen by the legislature thereof,*[3] for six years; and each Senator shall have one vote.

Immediately after they shall be assembled in consequence of the first election, they shall be divided as equally as may be into three classes. The seats of the Senators of the first class shall be vacated at the expiration of the second year, of the second class at the expiration of the fourth year, and the third class at the expiration of the sixth year, so that one third may be chosen every second year;[4] *and if vacancies happen by resignation, or otherwise, during the recess of the legislature of any State, the executive thereof may make temporary appointments until the next meeting of the legislature, which shall then fill such vacancies.*[5]

No person shall be a Senator who shall not have attained to the age of thirty years, and been nine years a citizen of the United States and who shall not, when elected, be an inhabitant of that State for which he shall be chosen.

The Vice President of the United States shall be President of the Senate, but shall have no vote, unless they be equally divided.

The Senate shall choose their other officers, and also a President pro tempore, in the absence of the Vice President, or when he shall exercise the office of President of the United States.

The Senate shall have the sole power to try all impeachments. When sitting for that purpose, they shall be on oath or affirmation.

---

[2] A temporary provision. There are currently 435 members of the House.
[3] See Seventeenth Amendment.
[4] Temporary method to begin the process of electing 1/3 of the Senate every two years.
[5] Method of filling vacancies changed by Seventeenth Amendment.

When the President of the United States is tried, the Chief Justice shall preside: And no person shall be convicted without the concurrence of two thirds of the members present.

Judgment in cases of impeachment shall not extend further than to removal from office, and disqualification to hold and enjoy any office of honor, trust or profit under the United States: but the party convicted shall nevertheless be liable and subject to indictment, trial, judgment and punishment, according to law.

SECTION 4. The times, places and manner of holding elections for Senators and Representatives, shall be prescribed in each State by the legislature thereof; but the Congress may at any time by law make or alter such regulations, except as to the places of choosing Senators.

The Congress shall assemble at least once in every year, and such meeting shall be on the *first Monday in December*, unless they shall by law appoint a different day.[6]

SECTION 5. Each House shall be the judge of the elections, returns and qualifications of its own members, and a majority of each shall constitute a quorum to do business; but a smaller number may adjourn from day to day, and may be authorized to compel the attendance of absent members, in such manner, and under such penalties as each House may provide.

Each House may determine the rules of its proceedings, punish its members for disorderly behavior, and, with the concurrence of two thirds, expel a member.

Each House shall keep a journal of its proceedings, and from time to time publish the same, excepting such parts as may in their judgment require secrecy; and the yeas and nays of the members of either House on any question shall, at the desire of one fifth of those present, be entered on the journal.

Neither House, during the session of Congress, shall, without the consent of the other, adjourn for more than three days, nor to any other place than that in which the two Houses shall be sitting.

SECTION 6. The Senators and Representatives shall receive a compensation for their services, to be ascertained by law, and paid out of

[6] Changed to January 3rd by Twentieth Amendment.

the treasury of the United States. They shall in all cases, except treason, felony and breach of the peace, be privileged from arrest during their attendance at the session of their respective Houses, and in going to and returning from the same; and for any speech or debate in either House, they shall not be questioned in any other place.

No Senator or Representative shall, during the time for which he was elected, be appointed to any civil office under the authority of the United States, which shall have been created, or the emoluments whereof shall have been increased during such time: and no person holding any office under the United States, shall be a member of either House during his continuance in office.

SECTION 7. All bills for raising revenue shall originate in the House of Representatives; but the Senate may propose or concur with amendments as on other Bills.

Every bill which shall have passed the House of Representatives and the Senate, shall, before it become a law, be presented to the President of the United States; if he approves he shall sign it, but if not he shall return it, with his objections to that House in which it shall have originated, who shall enter the objections at large on their journal, and proceed to reconsider it. If after such reconsideration two thirds of that House shall agree to pass the bill, it shall be sent, together with the objections, to the other House, by which it shall likewise be reconsidered, and if approved by two thirds of that House, it shall become a law. But in all such cases the votes of both Houses shall be determined by yeas and nays, and the names of the persons voting for and against the bill shall be entered on the journal of each House respectively. If any bill shall not be returned by the President within ten days (Sundays excepted) after it shall have been presented to him, the same shall be a law, in like manner as if he had signed it, unless the Congress by their adjournment prevent its return, in which case it shall not be a law.

Every order, resolution, or vote to which the concurrence of the Senate and House of Representatives may be necessary (except on a question of adjournment) shall be presented to the President of the United States; and before the same shall take effect, shall be approved by him, or being disapproved by him, shall be repassed by two thirds of the Senate and House of Representatives, according to the rules and limitations prescribed in the case of a bill.

SECTION 8. The Congress shall have power to lay and collect taxes, duties, imposts and excises, to pay the debts and provide for the common defense and general welfare of the United States; but all duties, imposts and excises shall be uniform throughout the United States;

To borrow money on the credit of the United States;

To regulate commerce with foreign nations, and among the several States, and with the Indian tribes;

To establish a uniform rule of naturalization, and uniform laws on the subject of bankruptcies throughout the United States;

To coin money, regulate the value thereof, and of foreign coin, and fix the standard of weights and measures;

To provide for the punishment of counterfeiting the securities and current coin of the United States;

To establish post offices and post roads;

To promote the progress of science and useful arts, by securing for limited times to authors and inventors the exclusive right to their respective writings and discoveries;

To constitute tribunals inferior to the Supreme Court;

To define and punish piracies and felonies committed on the high seas, and offenses against the law of nations;

To declare war, grant letters of marque and reprisal, and make rules concerning captures on land and water;

To raise and support armies, but no appropriation of money to that use shall be for a longer term than two years;

To provide and maintain a navy;

To make rules for the government and regulation of the land and naval forces;

To provide for calling forth the militia to execute the laws of the union, suppress insurrections and repel invasions;

To provide for organizing, arming, and disciplining, the militia, and for governing such part of them as may be employed in the service of the United States, reserving to the States respectively, the appointment of the officers, and the authority of training the militia according to the discipline prescribed by Congress;

To exercise exclusive legislation in all cases whatsoever, over such District (not exceeding ten miles square) as may, by cession of particular States, and the acceptance of Congress, become the seat of the government of the United States, and to exercise like authority over all places purchased by the consent of the legislature of the

State in which the same shall be, for the erection of forts, magazines, arsenals, dockyards, and other needful buildings; — And

To make all laws which shall be necessary and proper for carrying into execution the foregoing powers, and all other powers vested by this Constitution in the government of the United States, or in any department or officer thereof.

SECTION 9. *The migration or importation of such persons as any of the States now existing shall think proper to admit, shall not be prohibited by the Congress prior to the year one thousand eight hundred and eight, but a tax or duty may be imposed on such importation, not exceeding ten dollars for each person.*[7]

The privilege of the writ of habeas corpus shall not be suspended, unless when in cases of rebellion or invasion the public safety may require it.

No bill of attainder or ex post facto Law shall be passed.

No capitation, or other direct, tax shall be laid, unless in proportion to the census or enumeration herein before directed to be taken.[8]

No tax or duty shall be laid on articles exported from any State.

No preference shall be given by any regulation of commerce or revenue to the ports of one State over those of another: nor shall vessels bound to, or from, one State, be obliged to enter, clear or pay duties in another.

No money shall be drawn from the treasury, but in consequence of appropriations made by law; and a regular statement and account of receipts and expenditures of all public money shall be published from time to time.

No title of nobility shall be granted by the United States: and no person holding any office of profit or trust under them, shall, without the consent of the Congress, accept of any present, emolument, office, or title, of any kind whatever, from any king, prince, or foreign State.

SECTION 10. No State shall enter into any treaty, alliance, or confederation; grant letters of marque and reprisal; coin money; emit bills of credit; make anything but gold and silver coin a tender in

[7] Refers to slave trade which was allowed for first twenty years.
[8] See Sixteenth Amendment.

payment of debts; pass any bill of attainder, ex post facto law, or law impairing the obligation of contracts, or grant any title of nobility.

No State shall, without the consent of the Congress, lay any imposts or duties on imports or exports, except what may be absolutely necessary for executing its inspection laws: and the net produce of all duties and imposts, laid by any State on imports or exports, shall be for the use of the treasury of the United States; and all such laws shall be subject to the revision and control of the Congress.

No State shall, without the consent of Congress, lay any duty of tonnage, keep troops, or ships of war in time of peace, enter into any agreement or compact with another State, or with a foreign power, or engage in war, unless actually invaded, or in such imminent danger as will not admit of delay.

Article II

Section 1. The executive power shall be vested in a President of the United States of America. He shall hold his office during the term of four years, and, together with the Vice President, chosen for the same term, be elected, as follows:

Each State[9] shall appoint, in such manner as the Legislature thereof may direct, a number of electors, equal to the whole number of Senators and Representatives to which the State may be entitled in the Congress: but no Senator or Representative, or person holding an office of trust or profit under the United States, shall be appointed an elector.

The electors shall meet in their respective States, and vote by ballot for two persons, of whom one at least shall not be an inhabitant of the same State with themselves. And they shall make a list of all the persons voted for, and of the number of votes for each; which list they shall sign and certify, and transmit sealed to the seat of the government of the United States, directed to the President of the Senate. The President of the Senate shall, in the presence of the Senate and House of Representatives, open all the certificates, and the votes shall then be counted. The person having the greatest number of votes shall be the President, if such number be a majority of the whole number of electors appointed; and if there be more than

[9] District of Columbia added by twenty-third Amendment.

one who have such majority, and have an equal number of votes, then the House of Representatives shall immediately choose by ballot one of them for President; and if no person have a majority, then from the five highest on the list the said House shall in like manner choose the President. But in choosing the President, the votes shall be taken by States, the representation from each State having one vote; A quorum for this purpose shall consist of a member or members from two thirds of the States, and a majority of all the States shall be necessary to a choice. In every case, after the choice of the President, the person having the greatest number of votes of the electors shall be the Vice President. But if there should remain two or more who have equal votes, the Senate shall choose from them by ballot the Vice President. [10]

The Congress may determine the time of choosing the electors, and the day on which they shall give their votes; which day shall be the same throughout the United States.

No person except a natural born citizen, or a citizen of the United States, at the time of the adoption of this Constitution, shall be eligible to the office of President; neither shall any person be eligible to that office who shall not have attained to the age of thirty five years, and been fourteen Years a resident within the United States.

In case of the removal of the President from office, or of his death, resignation, or inability to discharge the powers and duties of the said office, the same shall devolve on the Vice President, and the Congress may by law provide for the case of removal, death, resignation or inability, both of the President and Vice President, declaring what officer shall then act as President, and such officer shall act accordingly, until the disability be removed, or a President shall be elected. [11]

The President shall, at stated times, receive for his services, a compensation, which shall neither be increased nor diminished during the period for which he shall have been elected, and he shall not receive within that period any other emolument from the United States, or any of them.

Before he enter on the execution of his office, he shall take the following oath or affirmation: — "I do solemnly swear (or affirm)

[10] Changed by Twelfth Amendment.
[11] See Twentieth and Twenty-fifth Amendments.

that I will faithfully execute the office of President of the United States, and will to the best of my ability, preserve, protect and defend the Constitution of the United States."

SECTION 2. The President shall be commander in chief of the Army and Navy of the United States, and of the militia of the several States, when called into the actual service of the United States; he may require the opinion, in writing, of the principal officer in each of the executive departments, upon any subject relating to the duties of their respective offices, and he shall have power to grant reprieves and pardons for offenses against the United States, except in cases of impeachment.

He shall have power, by and with the advice and consent of the Senate, to make treaties, provided two thirds of the Senators present concur; and he shall nominate, and by and with the advice and consent of the Senate, shall appoint ambassadors, other public ministers and consuls, judges of the Supreme Court, and all other officers of the United States, whose appointments are not herein otherwise provided for, and which shall be established by law: but the Congress may by law vest the appointment of such inferior officers, as they think proper, in the President alone, in the courts of law, or in the heads of departments.

The President shall have power to fill up all vacancies that may happen during the recess of the Senate, by granting commissions which shall expire at the end of their next session.

SECTION 3. He shall from time to time give to the Congress information of the state of the union, and recommend to their consideration such measures as he shall judge necessary and expedient; he may, on extraordinary occasions, convene both Houses, or either of them, and in case of disagreement between them, with respect to the time of adjournment, he may adjourn them to such time as he shall think proper; he shall receive ambassadors and other public ministers; he shall take care that the laws be faithfully executed, and shall commission all the officers of the United States.

SECTION 4. The President, Vice President and all civil officers of the United States, shall be removed from office on impeachment for, and conviction of, treason, bribery, or other high crimes and misdemeanors.

Article III

SECTION 1. The judicial power of the United States, shall be vested in one Supreme Court, and in such inferior courts as the Congress may from time to time ordain and establish. The judges, both of the supreme and inferior courts, shall hold their offices during good behaviour, and shall, at stated times, receive for their services, a compensation, which shall not be diminished during their continuance in office.

SECTION 2. The judicial power shall extend to all cases, in law and equity, arising under this Constitution, the laws of the United States, and treaties made, or which shall be made, under their authority; — to all cases affecting ambassadors, other public ministers and consuls; — to all cases of admiralty and maritime jurisdiction; — to controversies to which the United States shall be a party; — to controversies between two or more States; — between a State and citizens of another State; — between citizens of different States; — between citizens of the same State claiming lands under grants of different States, and between a State, or the citizens thereof, and foreign States, *citizens or subjects*.[12]

In all cases affecting ambassadors, other public ministers and consuls, and those in which a State shall be party, the Supreme Court shall have original jurisdiction. In all the other cases before mentioned, the Supreme Court shall have appellate jurisdiction, both as to law and fact, with such exceptions, and under such regulations as the Congress shall make.

The trial of all crimes, except in cases of impeachment, shall be by jury; and such trial shall be held in the State where the said crimes shall have been committed; but when not committed within any State, the trial shall be at such place or places as the Congress may by law have directed.

SECTION 3. Treason against the United States, shall consist only in levying war against them, or in adhering to their enemies, giving them aid and comfort. No person shall be convicted of treason unless on the testimony of two witnesses to the same overt act, or on confession in open court.

[12] Changed by Eleventh Amendment.

The Congress shall have power to declare the punishment of treason, but no attainder of treason shall work corruption of blood, or forfeiture except during the life of the person attainted.

Article IV

SECTION 1. Full faith and credit shall be given in each State to the public acts, records, and judicial proceedings of every other State. And the Congress may by general laws prescribe the manner in which such acts, records, and proceedings shall be proved, and the effect thereof.

SECTION 2. The citizens of each State shall be entitled to all privileges and immunities of citizens in the several States.

A person charged in any State with treason, felony, or other crime, who shall flee from justice, and be found in another State, shall on demand of the executive authority of the State from which he fled, be delivered up, to be removed to the State having jurisdiction of the crime.

No person held to service or labor in one State, under the laws thereof, escaping into another, shall, in consequence of any law or regulation therein, be discharged from such service or labor, but shall be delivered up on claim of the party to whom such service or labor may be due.[13]

SECTION 3. New States may be admitted by the Congress into this union; but no new States shall be formed or erected within the jurisdiction of any other State; nor any State be formed by the junction of two or more States, or parts of States, without the consent of the legislatures of the States concerned as well as of the Congress.

The Congress shall have power to dispose of and make all needful rules and regulations respecting the territory or other property belonging to the United States; and nothing in this Constitution shall be so construed as to prejudice any claims of the United States, or of any particular State.

SECTION 4. The United States shall guarantee to every State in this union a republican form of government, and shall protect each of

---

[13] Abolished by Thirteenth Amendment.

them against invasion; and on application of the legislature, or of the executive (when the legislature cannot be convened) against domestic violence.

Article V

The Congress, whenever two thirds of both houses shall deem it necessary, shall propose amendments to this Constitution, or, on the application of the legislatures of two thirds of the several States, shall call a convention for proposing amendments, which, in either case, shall be valid to all intents and purposes, as part of this Constitution, when ratified by the legislatures of three fourths of the several States, or by conventions in three fourths thereof, as the one or the other mode of ratification may be proposed by the Congress; provided *that no amendment which may be made prior to the year one thousand eight hundred and eight shall in any manner affect the first and fourth clauses in the ninth section of the first article; and* [14] that no State, without its consent, shall be deprived of its equal suffrage in the Senate.

Article VI

All debts contracted and engagements entered into, before the adoption of this Constitution, shall be as valid against the United States under this Constitution, as under the Confederation.

This Constitution, and the laws of the United States which shall be made in pursuance thereof; and all treaties made, or which shall be made, under the authority of the United States, shall be the supreme law of the land; and the judges in every State shall be bound thereby, anything in the Constitution or laws of any State to the contrary notwithstanding.

The Senators and Representatives before mentioned, and the members of the several State legislatures, and all executive and judicial officers, both of the United States and of the several States, shall be bound by oath or affirmation, to support this Constitution; but no religious test shall ever be required as a qualification to any office or public trust under the United States.

---

[14] Became obsolete in 1808.

Article VII

The ratification of the conventions of nine States, shall be sufficient for the establishment of this Constitution between the States so ratifying the same.

Done in convention by the unanimous consent of the States present the seventeenth day of September in the year of our Lord one thousand seven hundred and eighty seven and of the independence of the United States of America the twelfth. In witness whereof We have hereunto subscribed our Names.

http://memory.loc.gov/const/const.html Source of Text
http://www.archives.gov/exhibit_hall/charters_of_freedom/constitution/constitution_transcription.html
(US National Archives & Records Administration. Has a very nice interactive hyperlinked display in which highlighted portions of the Constitution changed by Amendment are linked to the text of the corresponding Amendment. In addition, there are biographies of each of the 39 signers.

The Preamble to

The Bill of Rights

Congress of the United States

begun and held at the City of New-York, on Wednesday the fourth of March, one thousand seven hundred and eighty nine.

THE Conventions of a number of the States, having at the time of their adopting the Constitution, expressed a desire, in order to prevent misconstruction or abuse of its powers, that further declaratory and restrictive clauses should be added: And as extending the ground of public confidence in the Government, will best ensure the beneficent ends of its institution.

RESOLVED by the Senate and House of Representatives of the United States of America, in Congress assembled, two thirds of both Houses concurring, that the following Articles be proposed to the Legislatures of the several States, as amendments to the Constitution of the United States, all, or any of which Articles, when ratified by three fourths of the said Legislatures, to be valid to all intents and purposes, as part of the said Constitution; viz.

ARTICLES in addition to, and Amendment of the Constitution of the United States of America, proposed by Congress, and ratified by the Legislatures of the several States, pursuant to the fifth Article of the original Constitution.

The source for the Preamable to the Bill of Rights is
http://www.archives.gov/exhibit_hall/charters_of_freedom/bill_of_rights/
preamble.html

THE BILL OF RIGHTS
Ratified by Congress 1791

Amendment I
Congress shall make no law respecting an establishment of religion, or prohibiting the free exercise thereof; or abridging the freedom of speech, or of the press, or the right of the people peaceably to assemble, and to petition the Government for a redress of grievances.

Amendment II
A well regulated Militia, being necessary to the security of a free State, the right of the people to keep and bear Arms, shall not be infringed.

Amendment III
No Soldier shall, in time of peace be quartered in any house, without the consent of the Owner, nor in time of war, but in a manner to be prescribed by law.

Amendment IV
The right of the people to be secure in their persons, houses, papers, and effects, against unreasonable searches and seizures, shall not be violated, and no Warrants shall issue, but upon probable cause, supported by Oath or affirmation, and particularly describing the place to be searched, and the persons or things to be seized.

Amendment V
No person shall be held to answer for a capital, or otherwise infamous crime, unless on a presentment or indictment of a Grand Jury, except in cases arising in the land or naval forces, or in the Militia, when in actual service in time of War or public danger; nor shall any person be subject for the same offense to be twice put in jeopardy of life or limb, nor shall be compelled in any criminal case to be a witness against himself, nor be deprived of life, liberty, or property, without due process of law; nor shall private property be taken for public use without just compensation.

Amendment VI

In all criminal prosecutions, the accused shall enjoy the right to a speedy and public trial, by an impartial jury of the State and district wherein the crime shall have been committed; which district shall have been previously ascertained by law, and to be informed of the nature and cause of the accusation; to be confronted with the witnesses against him; to have compulsory process for obtaining witnesses in his favor, and to have the assistance of counsel for his defense.

Amendment VII

In Suits at common law, where the value in controversy shall exceed twenty dollars, the right of trial by jury shall be preserved, and no fact tried by a jury shall be otherwise re-examined in any Court of the United States, than according to the rules of the common law.

Amendment VIII

Excessive bail shall not be required, nor excessive fines imposed, nor cruel and unusual punishments inflicted.

Amendment IX

The enumeration in the Constitution of certain rights shall not be construed to deny or disparage others retained by the people.

Amendment X

The powers not delegated to the United States by the Constitution, nor prohibited by it to the States, are reserved to the States respectively, or to the people.

THE BALANCE OF THE
CONSTITUTIONAL AMENDMENTS TO DATE

Amendment XI

Passed by Congress March 4, 1794. Ratified February 7, 1795. (Note: Article III, section 2, of the Constitution was modified by amendment 11.)

The Judicial power of the United States shall not be construed to extend to any suit in law or equity, commenced or prosecuted against one of the United States by Citizens of another State, or by Citizens or Subjects of any Foreign State.

Amendment XII

Passed by Congress December 9, 1803. Ratified June 15, 1804. (Note: A portion of Article II, section 1 of the Constitution was superseded by the 12th amendment.)

The Electors shall meet in their respective states and vote by ballot for President and Vice-President, one of whom, at least, shall not be an inhabitant of the same state with themselves; they shall name in their ballots the person voted for as President, and in distinct ballots the person voted for as Vice-President, and they shall make distinct lists of all persons voted for as President, and of all persons voted for as Vice-President, and of the number of votes for each, which lists they shall sign and certify, and transmit sealed to the seat of the government of the United States, directed to the President of the Senate; — the President of the Senate shall, in the presence of the Senate and House of Representatives, open all the certificates and the votes shall then be counted; — The person having the greatest number of votes for President, shall be the President, if such number be a majority of the whole number of Electors appointed; and if no person have such majority, then from the persons having the highest numbers not exceeding three on the list of those voted for as President, the House of Representatives shall choose immediately, by ballot, the President. But in choosing the President, the votes shall be taken by states, the representation from each state having one vote; a quorum for this purpose shall consist of a member or members from two-thirds of the states, and a majority of all the states shall be necessary to a choice. [And if the House of Representatives shall not choose a President whenever the right of choice shall devolve upon them, before the fourth day of March next following, then the Vice-President shall act as President, as in case of the death or other constitutional disability of the President. —]* The person having the greatest number of votes as Vice-President, shall be the Vice-President, if such number be a majority of the whole number of Electors appointed, and if no person have a majority, then from the two highest numbers on the list, the Senate shall choose the Vice-President; a quorum for the purpose shall consist of two-thirds of the whole number of Senators, and a majority of the whole number shall be necessary to a choice. But no person constitutionally ineligible to the office of President shall be eligible to that of Vice-President of the United States.

*Superseded by Section 3 of the 20th Amendment.

Amendment XIII

Passed by Congress January 31, 1865. Ratified December 6, 1865. (Note: A portion of Article IV, section 2, of the Constitution was superseded by the 13th amendment.)

SECTION 1.
Neither slavery nor involuntary servitude, except as a punishment for crime whereof the party shall have been duly convicted, shall exist within the United States, or any place subject to their jurisdiction.
SECTION 2.
Congress shall have power to enforce this article by appropriate legislation.

Amendment XIV

Passed by Congress June 13, 1866. Ratified July 9, 1868. (Note: Article I, section 2, of the Constitution was modified by section 2 of the 14th amendment.)

SECTION 1.
All persons born or naturalized in the United States, and subject to the jurisdiction thereof, are citizens of the United States and of the State wherein they reside. No State shall make or enforce any law which shall abridge the privileges or immunities of citizens of the United States; nor shall any State deprive any person of life, liberty,

or property, without due process of law; nor deny to any person within its jurisdiction the equal protection of the laws.

SECTION 2.

Representatives shall be apportioned among the several States according to their respective numbers, counting the whole number of persons in each State, excluding Indians not taxed. But when the right to vote at any election for the choice of electors for President and Vice-President of the United States, Representatives in Congress, the Executive and Judicial officers of a State, or the members of the Legislature thereof, is denied to any of the male inhabitants of such State, being twenty-one years of age,* and citizens of the United States, or in any way abridged, except for participation in rebellion, or other crime, the basis of representation therein shall be reduced in the proportion which the number of such male citizens shall bear to the whole number of male citizens twenty-one years of age in such State.

SECTION 3.

No person shall be a Senator or Representative in Congress, or elector of President and Vice-President, or hold any office, civil or military, under the United States, or under any State, who, having previously taken an oath, as a member of Congress, or as an officer of the United States, or as a member of any State legislature, or as an executive or judicial officer of any State, to support the Constitution of the United States, shall have engaged in insurrection or rebellion against the same, or given aid or comfort to the enemies thereof. But Congress may by a vote of two-thirds of each House, remove such disability.

SECTION 4.

The validity of the public debt of the United States, authorized by law, including debts incurred for payment of pensions and bounties for services in suppressing insurrection or rebellion, shall not be questioned. But neither the United States nor any State shall assume or pay any debt or obligation incurred in aid of insurrection or rebellion against the United States, or any claim for the loss or emancipation of any slave; but all such debts, obligations and claims shall be held illegal and void.

SECTION 5.
The Congress shall have the power to enforce, by appropriate legislation, the provisions of this article.

Changed by section 1 of the 26th amendment.

Amendment XV

Passed by Congress February 26, 1869. Ratified February 3, 1870.

SECTION 1.
The right of citizens of the United States to vote shall not be denied or abridged by the United States or by any State on account of race, color, or previous condition of servitude.

SECTION 2.
The Congress shall have the power to enforce this article by appropriate legislation.

Amendment XVI

Passed by Congress July 2, 1909. Ratified February 3, 1913. (Note: Article I, section 9, of the Constitution was modified by amendment 16.)

The Congress shall have power to lay and collect taxes on incomes, from whatever source derived, without apportionment among the several States, and without regard to any census or enumeration.

Amendment XVII

Passed by Congress May 13, 1912. Ratified April 8, 1913. (Note: Article I, section 3, of the Constitution was modified by the 17th amendment.)

The Senate of the United States shall be composed of two Senators from each State, elected by the people thereof, for six years; and each Senator shall have one vote. The electors in each State shall have the qualifications requisite for electors of the most numerous branch of the State legislatures.

When vacancies happen in the representation of any State in the Senate, the executive authority of such State shall issue writs of election to fill such vacancies: Provided, That the legislature of any State may empower the executive thereof to make temporary appointments until the people fill the vacancies by election as the legislature may direct.

This amendment shall not be so construed as to affect the election or term of any Senator chosen before it becomes valid as part of the Constitution.

Amendment XVIII

Passed by Congress December 18, 1917. Ratified January 16, 1919. (Repealed by Amendment 21.)

SECTION 1.
After one year from the ratification of this article the manufacture, sale, or transportation of intoxicating liquors within, the importation thereof into, or the exportation thereof from the United States and all territory subject to the jurisdiction thereof for beverage purposes is hereby prohibited.

SECTION 2.
The Congress and the several States shall have concurrent power to enforce this article by appropriate legislation.

SECTION 3.
This article shall be inoperative unless it shall have been ratified as an amendment to the Constitution by the legislatures of the several States, as provided in the Constitution, within seven years from the date of the submission hereof to the States by the Congress.

Amendment XIX

Passed by Congress June 4, 1919. Ratified August 18, 1920.

The right of citizens of the United States to vote shall not be denied or abridged by the United States or by any State on account of sex.

Congress shall have power to enforce this article by appropriate legislation.

Amendment XX

Passed by Congress March 2, 1932. Ratified January 23, 1933. (Note: Article I, section 4, of the Constitution was modified by section 2 of this amendment. In addition, a portion of the 12th amendment was superseded by section 3.)

SECTION 1.

The terms of the President and the Vice President shall end at noon on the 20th day of January, and the terms of Senators and Representatives at noon on the 3rd day of January, of the years in which such terms would have ended if this article had not been ratified; and the terms of their successors shall then begin.

SECTION 2.

The Congress shall assemble at least once in every year, and such meeting shall begin at noon on the 3rd day of January, unless they shall by law appoint a different day.

SECTION 3.

If, at the time fixed for the beginning of the term of the President, the President elect shall have died, the Vice President elect shall become President. If a President shall not have been chosen before the time fixed for the beginning of his term, or if the President elect shall have failed to qualify, then the Vice President elect shall act as President until a President shall have qualified; and the Congress may by law provide for the case wherein neither a President elect nor a Vice President shall have qualified, declaring who shall then act as President, or the manner in which one who is to act shall be selected, and such person shall act accordingly until a President or Vice President shall have qualified.

SECTION 4.

The Congress may by law provide for the case of the death of any of the persons from whom the House of Representatives may choose a President whenever the right of choice shall have devolved upon them, and for the case of the death of any of the persons from whom the Senate may choose a Vice President whenever the right of choice shall have devolved upon them.

SECTION 5.

Sections 1 and 2 shall take effect on the 15th day of October following the ratification of this article.

SECTION 6.

This article shall be inoperative unless it shall have been ratified as an amendment to the Constitution by the legislatures of three-fourths of the several States within seven years from the date of its submission.

Amendment XXI

Passed by Congress February 20, 1933. Ratified December 5, 1933.

SECTION 1.
The eighteenth article of amendment to the Constitution of the United States is hereby repealed.

SECTION 2.
The transportation or importation into any State, Territory, or Possession of the United States for delivery or use therein of intoxicating liquors, in violation of the laws thereof, is hereby prohibited.

SECTION 3.
This article shall be inoperative unless it shall have been ratified as an amendment to the Constitution by conventions in the several States, as provided in the Constitution, within seven years from the date of the submission hereof to the States by the Congress.

Amendment XXII

Passed by Congress March 21, 1947. Ratified February 27, 1951.

SECTION 1.
No person shall be elected to the office of the President more than twice, and no person who has held the office of President, or acted as President, for more than two years of a term to which some other person was elected President shall be elected to the office of President more than once. But this Article shall not apply to any person holding the office of President when this Article was proposed by Congress, and shall not prevent any person who may be holding the office of President, or acting as President, during the term within which this Article becomes operative from holding the office of President or acting as President during the remainder of such term.

SECTION 2.
This article shall be inoperative unless it shall have been ratified as an amendment to the Constitution by the legislatures of three-

fourths of the several States within seven years from the date of its submission to the States by the Congress.

Amendment XXIII

Passed by Congress June 16, 1960. Ratified March 29, 1961.

SECTION 1.
The District constituting the seat of Government of the United States shall appoint in such manner as Congress may direct:

A number of electors of President and Vice President equal to the whole number of Senators and Representatives in Congress to which the District would be entitled if it were a State, but in no event more than the least populous State; they shall be in addition to those appointed by the States, but they shall be considered, for the purposes of the election of President and Vice President, to be electors appointed by a State; and they shall meet in the District and perform such duties as provided by the twelfth article of amendment.

SECTION 2.
The Congress shall have power to enforce this article by appropriate legislation.

Amendment XXIV

Passed by Congress August 27, 1962. Ratified January 23, 1964.

SECTION 1.
The right of citizens of the United States to vote in any primary or other election for President or Vice President, for electors for President or Vice President, or for Senator or Representative in Congress, shall not be denied or abridged by the United States or any State by reason of failure to pay poll tax or other tax.

SECTION 2.
The Congress shall have power to enforce this article by appropriate legislation.

Amendment XXV

Passed by Congress July 6, 1965. Ratified February 10, 1967. (Note: Article II, section 1, of the Constitution was affected by the 25th amendment.)

SECTION 1.

In case of the removal of the President from office or of his death or resignation, the Vice President shall become President.

SECTION 2.

Whenever there is a vacancy in the office of the Vice President, the President shall nominate a Vice President who shall take office upon confirmation by a majority vote of both Houses of Congress.

SECTION 3.

Whenever the President transmits to the President pro tempore of the Senate and the Speaker of the House of Representatives his written declaration that he is unable to discharge the powers and duties of his office, and until he transmits to them a written declaration to the contrary, such powers and duties shall be discharged by the Vice President as Acting President.

SECTION 4.

Whenever the Vice President and a majority of either the principal officers of the executive departments or of such other body as Congress may by law provide, transmit to the President pro tempore of the Senate and the Speaker of the House of Representatives their written declaration that the President is unable to discharge the powers and duties of his office, the Vice President shall immediately assume the powers and duties of the office as Acting President.

Thereafter, when the President transmits to the President pro tempore of the Senate and the Speaker of the House of Representatives his written declaration that no inability exists, he shall resume the powers and duties of his office unless the Vice President and a majority of either the principal officers of the executive department or of such other body as Congress may by law provide, transmit within four days to the President pro tempore of the Senate and the Speaker of the House of Representatives their written declaration that the President is unable to discharge the powers and duties of his office. Thereupon Congress shall decide the issue, assembling within forty-eight hours for that purpose if not in session. If the Congress, within twenty-one days after receipt of the latter written declaration, or, if Congress is not in session, within twenty-one days after Congress is required to assemble, determines by two-thirds vote of both Houses that the President is unable to discharge the powers and duties of his office, the Vice President shall continue to discharge the same as Acting President; otherwise, the President shall resume the powers and duties of his office.

Amendment XXVI

Passed by Congress March 23, 1971. Ratified July 1, 1971. (Note: Amendment 14, section 2, of the Constitution was modified by section 1 of the 26th amendment.)

SECTION 1.
The right of citizens of the United States, who are eighteen years of age or older, to vote shall not be denied or abridged by the United States or by any State on account of age.

SECTION 2.
The Congress shall have power to enforce this article by appropriate legislation.

Amendment XXVII

Originally proposed Sept. 25, 1789. Ratified May 7, 1992.)

No law, varying the compensation for the services of the Senators and Representatives, shall take effect, until an election of representatives shall have intervened.

The Source of the Notes and ratification data above is the US National Archives and Records Administration:
http://www.archives.gov/exhibit_hall/charters_of_freedom/constitution/amendments_11-27.html

APPENDIX TWO

The Language of Tyranny

*It is not new. It is, in fact, man's second oldest faith. Its promise
was whispered in the first days of the Creation under the Tree of
the Knowledge of Good and Evil: "Ye shall be as gods." It is the
great alternative faith of mankind. Like all great faiths, its force
derives from a simple vision . . . The Communist vision is the
vision of Man without God.*

    *It is the vision of man's mind displacing God as the creative
intelligence of the world. . . . It is the vision of materialism.*
— Whittaker Chambers, *Witness*

The United Nations (UN) was founded in San Francisco in 1945
at a meeting chaired by an American traitor, Communist spy,
and Soviet espionage agent named Alger Hiss (later imprisoned).
Hiss served as the organization's first Secretary General, having been
recommended for that post by Soviet ambassador Andrei Gromyko.

    The utopian pipedream outlined in the opening paragraphs of
the UN Charter is followed by its Universal Declaration of Human
Rights. This presents a laundry list of "rights" among which are the
"right" to paid vacations and the "right" to hold opinions. The net
effect of this language is to so dilute the meaning of the word "rights"
that the word "rights" becomes meaningless. I do not believe this
was done by accident.

    True individual rights are inviolate. If I have the right to free
speech, you have the right to free speech. My rights do not lessen or
negate your rights. If I can assemble, you can assemble; if I can be
armed, you can be armed; if my house is secure from warrantless
searches, your house is secure from warrantless searches, and so forth.
Privileges are different. If I have the privilege of free speech, you can
tell me not to say things that bother you. If you have the privilege to
bear arms, I can tell you not to own scary looking ones that make me
feel anxious. If I have the privilege to be secure in my home against
warrantless searches, you can perform "sneak and peek" secret raids,
or tell me that since I live in public housing, or am driving my car on

a public road, you can search my apartment or vehicle anytime you decide.

According to America's founders, human beings are endowed by our Creator with unalienable rights. The meaning of "unalienable" is "incapable of being alienated, surrendered or transferred." They are protected *from* the state under the U.S. Constitution.

What the UN offers — as will be demonstrated in its own words in the following documents — are "alienable" rights, i.e. privileges, granted *by* the state, that can legally and arbitrarily be taken away whenever the state decides there is "good" reason. Quoting the exact wording of the International Covenant on Civil and Political Rights, "The above-mentioned rights shall not be subject to any restrictions except those which are provided by law, are necessary to protect national security, public order *(ordre public)*, public health or morals or the rights and freedoms of others, and are consistent with the other rights recognized in the present Covenant." That oft-repeated caveat may be described as the *conceptual antithesis of unalienable rights*.

I read the UN material for the first time because of a book on globalism. The author happened to quote the UN caveat mentioned above. I thought to myself, "I've finally got you, you right wing lunatic! It is unimaginable that anyone could openly make that statement." I went on to UN websites, made sure I got the "official versions," and to my shock learned the writer was not a lunatic, and that the people who wrote this material were not what I would call "my kind of people."

I also understood that probably very few of those who claim they support the UN (including many of my friends) have actually read its founding material.

Who, in his right mind, would be supportive of a political system that intended to replace his unalienable rights with alienable privileges?

That's actually why I put this book together. I am convinced that intelligent people will make intelligent decisions once they have seen the facts. I hope this assumption is correct.

The only solution, in my opinion, to maintaining our freedom is to withdraw from membership in the UN and evict it from New York City. One wag suggested relocating the UN to Jerusalem, and making Jerusalem an international city open to Jews, Christians, and Muslims equally, and administering it and its holy sites under UN auspices. Not only would that give the UN a manageable area in which to practice the art of government, it would help solve the chronic problem of unpaid parking tickets in New York City.

I am going to make an uncharacteristically generous statement about the UN Applying the principles expressed in the following documents to a Third World kleptocracy like Haiti or Liberia, a Communist tyranny like Red China, or a Religious dictatorship like Iran, might actually yield, in the short run, a compassionate improvement for the victims of those forms of rule. Even the social-ist states of Europe might notice little change in their characteristi-cally disordered political lives.

But the principles proposed in the following pages are fatal to that greatest of advance in the history of political freedom on earth still alive in America. Thus America is caught in the cross hairs of every would-be tyrant stalking the earth, whether at home or abroad. For they well understand that the freedoms we enjoy are inimical to the world dictatorship they seek.

In presenting the following material I have attempted to limit myself to typographically highlighting (through the use of italics) certain statements that I consider either (a) fundamentally flawed in reason; (b) totally outside the scope of the values upon which Amer-ica was founded; or (c) so utterly untrustworthy, vague, and open to interpretation, as to be easily liable to abuse by tyrants. Occasional-ly I have footnoted certain statements with comments that I have tried to keep to a minimum in order not to insult the intelligence of the reader, which I believe will be insulted enough by reading what follows.

CHARTER OF THE UNITED NATIONS

June 26, 1945

Preamble

WE THE PEOPLES of the United Nations Determined

TO SAVE succeeding generations from the scourge of war, which twice in our lifetime has brought untold sorrow to mankind, and

TO REAFFIRM faith in fundamental human rights, in the dignity and worth of the human person, in the equal rights of men and women and of nations large and small, and

TO ESTABLISH conditions under which justice and respect for the obligations arising from treaties and other sources of international law can be maintained, and

TO PROMOTE social progress and better standards of life in larger freedom,

AND FOR THESE ENDS

TO PRACTICE tolerance and live together in peace with one another as good neighbors, and

TO UNITE our strength to maintain international peace and security, and

TO ENSURE by the acceptance of principles and the institution of methods, that armed force shall not be used, save in the common interest, and

TO EMPLOY international machinery for the promotion of the economic and social advancement of all peoples,

HAVE RESOLVED to Combine our Efforts to Accomplish these Aims

ACCORDINGLY, our respective Governments, through representatives assembled in the city of San Francisco, who have exhibited their full powers found to be in good and due form, have agreed to the present Charter of the United Nations and do hereby establish an international organization to be known as the United Nations.

CHAPTER I

PURPOSES AND PRINCIPLES

Article 1

The Purposes of the United Nations are:

1. To maintain international peace and security, and to that end: to take effective collective measures for the prevention and removal of threats to the peace, and for the suppression of acts of aggression or other breaches of the peace, and to bring about by peaceful means, and in conformity with the principles of justice and international law, adjustment or settlement of international disputes or situations which might lead to a breach of the peace;

2. To develop friendly relations among nations based on respect for the principle of equal rights and self-determination of peoples, and to take other appropriate measures to strengthen universal peace;

3. To achieve international cooperation in solving international problems of an economic, social, cultural, or humanitarian character, and in promoting and encouraging respect for human rights and for fundamental freedoms for all without distinction as to race, sex, language, or religion; and

4. To be a center for harmonizing the actions of nations in the attainment of these common ends.

Article 2

The Organization and its Members, in pursuit of the Purposes stated in Article 1, shall act in accordance with the following Principles.

1. The Organization is based on the principle of the sovereign equality of all its Members.

2. All Members, in order to ensure to all of them the rights and benefits resulting from membership, shall fulfill in good faith the obligations assumed by them in accordance with the present Charter.

3. All Members shall settle their international disputes by peaceful means in such a manner that international peace and security, and justice, are not endangered.

4. All Members shall refrain in their international relations from the threat or use of force against the territorial integrity or political independence of any state, or in any other manner inconsistent with the Purposes of the United Nations.

5. All Members shall give the United Nations every assistance in any action it takes in accordance with the present Charter, and shall refrain from giving assistance to any state against which the United Nations is taking preventive or enforcement action.

6. The Organization shall ensure that states which are not Members of the United Nations act in accordance with these Principles so far as may be necessary for the maintenance of international peace and security.

7. Nothing contained in the present Charter shall authorize the United Nations to intervene in matters which are essentially within the domestic jurisdiction of any state or shall require the Members to submit such matters to settlement under the present Charter; but this principle shall not prejudice the application of enforcement measures under Chapter VII.

[This excerpt from the idealistic sounding opening of the Charter is included to avoid the charge of not having included it. The balance of the text sets forth the organizational workings of the UN as a prototypical world government. The complete text of this document may be found at many locations on the Web including: http://www.hrweb.org/legal/unchartr.html

The United Nations
Universal Declaration of Human Rights

Adopted and proclaimed by General Assembly resolution 217 A (III) of 10 December 1948

Preamble

WHEREAS recognition of the inherent dignity and of the equal and inalienable rights[1] of all members of the human family is the foundation of freedom, justice, and peace in the world,

WHEREAS disregard and contempt for human rights have resulted in barbarous acts which have outraged the conscience of mankind, and the advent of a world in which human beings shall enjoy freedom of speech and belief and freedom from fear and want has been proclaimed as the highest aspiration of the common people,

WHEREAS it is essential, if man is not to be compelled to have recourse, as a last resort, to rebellion against tyranny and oppression, that human right should be protected by the rule of law,

WHEREAS the people of the United Nations have in the Charter rearmed their faith in fundamental human rights, in the dignity and worth of the human person and in the equal rights of men and women and have determined to promote social progress and better standards of life in larger freedom,

WHEREAS Member States have pledged themselves to achieve, in cooperation with the United Nations, the promotion of universal respect for and observance of human rights and fundamental freedoms,

WHEREAS a common understanding of these rights and freedoms is of the greatest importance for the full realization of this pledge,

Now, THEREFORE The General Assembly

---

[1] Take a look at Article 29 to see what the UN pretends to mean by "inalienable."

PROCLAIMS this Universal Declaration of Human Rights as a common standard of achievement for all peoples and all nations, to the end that *every individual and every organ of society, keeping this Declaration constantly in mind,* shall strive by teaching and education to promote respect for these rights and freedoms and by progressive measures, national and international to secure their universal and effective recognition and observance, both among the peoples of Member States themselves and among, the peoples of territories under their jurisdiction.

Article 1

All human beings are born free and equal in dignity and rights. They are endowed with reason and conscience and *should act* towards one another in a spirit of brotherhood.

Article 2

Everyone is entitled to all the rights and freedoms set forth in this declaration, without distinction of any kind, such as race, colour, sex, language, religion, political or other opinion, national or social origin, property, birth or other status.

Furthermore, no distinction shall be made on the basis of the political, jurisdictional or international status of the country or territory to which a person belongs, whether it be independent, trust, non-self-governing or under any other limitation of sovereignty.

Article 3

Everyone has the right to life, liberty and the *security of person*.

Article 4

No one shall be held in slavery or servitude; slavery and the slave trade shall be prohibited in all their forms.

Article 5

No one shall be subjected to torture or to cruel, inhuman or degrading treatment or punishment.

Article 6

Everyone has the right to recognition everywhere as a person before the law.

Article 7

All are equal before the law and are entitled without any discrimination to equal protection of the law. All are entitled to equal protection against any discrimination in violation of this Declaration and against any incitement to such discrimination.

Article 8

Everyone has the right to an effective remedy by the competent national tribunals for acts violating the fundamental right granted him by the constitution or by law.[2]

Article 9

No one shall be subject to arbitrary arrest, detention or exile.

Article 10

Everyone is entitled in full equality to a fair and public hearing by an independent and impartial tribunal in the determination of his rights and obligations and of any criminal charge against him.

Article 11

1. Everyone charged with a penal offense has the right to be presumed innocent until proved guilty according to law in a public trial at which he had all the guarantees necessary for his defense.

---

[2] Please note this unequivocal admission of exactly who or what is the source of the "rights" recognized by the UN. Note that it contradicts the word "inalienable" in first paragraph of the Preamble to this declaration. Finally, please compare it to Thomas Jefferson's immortal words in The Declaration of Independence reproduced in appendix one. Under which system would you prefer to live?

2. No one shall be held guilty of any penal offense on account of any act or omission which did not constitute a penal offense under national or international law, at the time when it was committed. Nor shall a heavier penalty be imposed than the one that was applicable at the time the penal offense was committed.

Article 12

No one shall be subject to arbitrary interference with his privacy, family, home or correspondence, nor to attacks upon his honour and reputation. Everyone has the right to the protection of the law against such interference or attacks.

Article 13

1. Everyone has the right to freedom of movement and residence within the borders of each state.

2. Everyone has the right to leave any country, including his own, and to return to his country.

Article 14

1. Everyone has the right to seek and to enjoy in other countries asylum from persecution.

2. This right may not be invoked in the case of prosecution genuinely arising from nonpolitical crimes or from acts contrary to the purposes and principles of the United Nations.

Article 15

1. Everyone has the right to a nationality.

2. No one shall be arbitrarily deprived of his nationality nor denied the right to change his nationality.

Article 16

Men and women of full age, without any limitation due to race, nationality or religion, have the right to marry and to found a family. They are entitled to equal rights as to marriage, *during marriage*[3] and at its dissolution.

Article 17

1. Everyone has the right to own property alone as well as in association with others.

2. No one shall be arbitrarily deprived of his property.

Article 18

Everyone has the right to freedom of thought, conscience and religion; this right includes freedom to change his religion or belief, and freedom, either alone or in community with others and in public or private, to manifest his religion or belief in teaching, practice, worship and observance.

Article 19

Everyone has the right to freedom of opinion and expression; this right includes freedom to hold opinions without interference and to seek, receive and impart information and ideas through any media and regardless of frontiers.

Article 20

1. Everyone has the right to freedom of peaceful assembly and association.

2. No one may be compelled to belong to an association.

---

[3] One can only imagine how they intend to enforce this one.

Article 21

1. Everyone has the right to take part in the government of his country, directly or through freely chosen representatives.

2. Everyone has the right of equal access to public service in his country.

3. The will of the people shall be basis of the authority of government; this will shall be expressed in the periodic and genuine elections which shall be by universal and equal suffrage and shall be held by secret vote or by equivalent free voting procedures.

Article 22

Everyone, as a member of society, has *the right to social security* and is entitled to realization, through national effort and international cooperation and in accordance with the organization and resources of each State of the economic, social and cultural rights indispensable for his dignity and the free development of his personality.

Article 23

1. Everyone has *the right to work,* to free choice of employment, to just and favourable conditions of work and to protection against unemployment.

2. Everyone, without any discrimination, has *the right to equal pay for equal work.*

3. Everyone who works has the right to just and favourable remuneration ensuring for himself and his family an existence worthy of human dignity, *and supplemented, if necessary, by other means of social protection.*

4. Everyone has the right to form and to join trade for the protection of his interests.

Article 24

Everyone has the right to rest and leisure including reasonable limitation of working hours and *periodic holidays with pay*.

Article 25

1. *Everyone has the right to a standard of living adequate for the health and well-being of himself and of his family, including food, clothing, housing and medical care and necessary social services, and the right to security in the event of unemployment, sickness, disability, widowhood, old age or other lack of livelihood in circumstances beyond his control.*

2. Motherhood and childhood are entitled to special care and assistance. All children, whether born in or out of wedlock, shall enjoy the same social protection.

Article 26

1. Everyone has the right to education. Education shall be free, at least in the elementary and fundamental stages. *Elementary education shall be compulsory.* Technical and professional education shall be made generally available and higher education shall be equally accessible to all on the basis of merit.

2. Education shall be directed to the full development of the human personality and to the strengthening of respect for human rights and fundamental freedoms. It shall promote understanding, tolerance and friendship among all nations, racial or religious groups, *and shall further the activities of the United Nations for the maintenance of peace.*

3. Parents have a prior right to choose the kind of education that shall be given to their children.

Article 27

1. Everyone has the right freely to participate in the cultural life of the community, to enjoy the arts and to share in scientific advancement and its benefits.

2. Everyone has the right to the protection of the moral and material interests resulting from any scientific, literary or artistic production of which he is the author.

Article 28

Everyone is entitled to a social and international order in which the rights and freedoms set forth in this Declaration can be fully realized.

Article 29

1. *Everyone has duties to the community in which alone the free and full development of his personality is possible.*

2. *In the exercise of his rights and freedoms, everyone shall be subject only to such limitations as are determined by law solely for the purpose of securing due recognition and respect for the rights and freedoms of others and of meeting the just requirements of morality, public order and the general welfare in a democratic society.*

3. These rights and freedoms may in no case be exercised contrary to the purposes and principles of the United Nations.

Article 30

Nothing in this Declaration may be interpreted as implying for any State, group or persons any right to engage in any activity or to perform any act aimed at the destruction of any of the rights and freedoms set forth herein.

This is the complete text of this document which may be found at many locations on the Web including: http://www.un.org/Overview/rights.html

International Covenant on Civil and Political Rights

Adopted and opened for signature, ratification and accession by General Assembly resolution 2200A (XXI) of 16 December 1966. Entry into force 23 March 1976, in accordance with Article 49

Preamble

The States Parties to the present Covenant,

Considering that, in accordance with the principles proclaimed in the Charter of the United Nations, recognition of the inherent dignity and of the equal and inalienable rights of all members of the human family is the foundation of freedom, justice and peace in the world,

Recognizing that *these rights derive from the inherent dignity of the human person,*

Recognizing that, in accordance with the Universal Declaration of Human Rights, the ideal of free human beings enjoying civil and political freedom and freedom from fear and want can only be achieved if conditions are created whereby everyone may enjoy his civil and political rights, as well as his economic, social and cultural rights,

Considering the obligation of States under the Charter of the United Nations to promote universal respect for, and observance of, human rights and freedoms,

Realizing *that the individual, having duties to other individuals and to the community to which he belongs, is under a responsibility to strive for the promotion and observance of the rights recognized in the present Covenant,*

Agree upon the following articles:

PART I

Article 1

1. All peoples have the right of self-determination. By virtue of that right they freely determine their political status and freely pursue their economic, social and cultural development.

2. All peoples may, for their own ends, freely dispose of their natural wealth and resources without prejudice to any obligations arising out of international economic co-operation, based upon the principle of mutual benefit, and international law. In no case may a people be deprived of its own means of subsistence.

3. The States Parties to the present Covenant, including those having responsibility for the administration of Non-Self-Governing and Trust Territories, shall promote the realization of the right of self-determination, and shall respect that right, in conformity with the provisions of the Charter of the United Nations.

PART II

Article 2

1. Each State Party to the present Covenant undertakes to respect and to ensure to all individuals within its territory and subject to its jurisdiction the rights recognized in the present Covenant, without distinction of any kind, such as race, colour, sex, language, religion, political or other opinion, national or social origin, property, birth or other status.

2. Where not already provided for by existing legislative or other measures, each State Party to the present Covenant undertakes to take the necessary steps in accordance with its constitutional processes and with the provisions of the present Covenant, to adopt such legislative or other measures as may be necessary to give effect to the rights recognized in the present Covenant.

3. Each State Party to the present Covenant undertakes:

    (a) To ensure that any person whose rights or freedoms as herein recognized are violated shall have an effective remedy, notwithstanding that the violation has been committed by persons acting in an official capacity;

    (b) To ensure that any person claiming such a remedy shall have his rights thereto determined by competent judicial, administrative or legislative authorities, or by any other competent authority provided for by the legal system of the State, and to develop the possibilities of judicial remedy;

    (c) To ensure that the competent authorities shall enforce such remedies when granted.

Article 3

The States Parties to the present Covenant undertake to ensure the equal right of men and women to the enjoyment of all civil and political rights set forth in the present Covenant.

Article 4

1. *In time of public emergency which threatens the life of the nation and the existence of which is officially proclaimed, the States Parties to the present Covenant may take measures derogating from their obligations under the present Covenant to the extent strictly required by the exigencies of the situation,* provided that such measures are not inconsistent with their other obligations under international law and do not involve discrimination solely on the ground of race, colour, sex, language, religion or social origin.

2. No derogation from articles 6, 7, 8 (paragraphs 1 and 2), 11, 15, 16 and 18 may be made under this provision.

3. Any State Party to the present Covenant availing itself of the right of derogation shall immediately inform the other States Parties to the present Covenant, through the intermediary of the Secretary-General of the United Nations, of the provisions from which it has derogated and of the reasons by which it was actuated. A further communication shall be made, through the same intermediary, on the date on which it terminates such derogation.

Article 5

1. Nothing in the present Covenant may be interpreted as implying for any State, group or person any right to engage in any activity or perform any act aimed at the destruction of any of the rights and freedoms recognized herein or at their limitation to a greater extent than is provided for in the present Covenant.

2. There shall be no restriction upon or derogation from any of the fundamental human rights recognized or existing in any State Party to the present Covenant pursuant to law, conventions, regulations or custom on the pretext that the present Covenant does not recognize such rights or that it recognizes them to a lesser extent.[1]

PART III

Article 6

1. Every human being has the inherent *right to life*. This right shall be protected by law. No one shall be arbitrarily deprived of his life.

2. In countries which have not abolished the death penalty, sentence of death may be imposed only for the most serious crimes in accordance with the law in force at the time of the commission of the crime and not contrary to the provisions of the present Covenant and to the Convention on the Prevention and Punishment of the Crime of Genocide. This penalty can only be carried out pursuant to a final judgment rendered by a competent court.

3. When deprivation of life constitutes the crime of genocide, it is understood that nothing in this article shall authorize any State Party to the present Covenant to derogate in any way from any obligation assumed under the provisions of the Convention on the Prevention and Punishment of the Crime of Genocide.

---

[1] Does this mean that America will retain our Second Amendment rights despite Kofi Annan's campaign against it as discussed in "Pulling Liberty's Teeth?"

4. Anyone sentenced to death shall have the right to seek pardon or commutation of the sentence. Amnesty, pardon or commutation of the sentence of death may be granted in all cases.

5. Sentence of death shall not be imposed for crimes committed by persons below eighteen years of age and shall not be carried out on pregnant women.

6. Nothing in this article shall be invoked to delay or to prevent the abolition of capital punishment by any State Party to the present Covenant.

Article 7

No one shall be subjected to torture or to cruel, inhuman or degrading treatment or punishment. In particular, no one shall be subjected without his free consent to medical or scientific experimentation.

Article 8

1. No one shall be held in slavery; slavery and the slave-trade in all their forms shall be prohibited.

2. No one shall be held in servitude.

3.
   (a) No one shall be required to perform forced or compulsory labour;
   (b) Paragraph 3(a) shall not be held to preclude, in countries where imprisonment with hard labour may be imposed as a punishment for a crime, the performance of hard labour in pursuance of a sentence to such punishment by a competent court;
   (c) For the purpose of this paragraph *the term "forced or compulsory labour" shall not include:*
      (i) Any work or service, not referred to in subparagraph (b), normally required of a person who is under detention in consequence of a lawful order of a court, or of a person during conditional release from such detention;

> (ii) Any service of a military character and, in countries where conscientious objection is recognized, any national service required by law of conscientious objectors;
>
> (iii) Any service exacted in cases of emergency or calamity threatening the life or well-being of the community;
>
> (iv) *Any work or service which forms part of normal civil obligations.*[3]

Article 9

1. Everyone has the right to liberty and security of person. No one shall be subjected to arbitrary arrest or detention. No one shall be deprived of his liberty except on such grounds and in accordance with such procedure as are established by law.

2. Anyone who is arrested shall be informed, at the time of arrest, of the reasons for his arrest and shall be promptly informed of any charges against him.

3. Anyone arrested or detained on a criminal charge shall be brought promptly before a judge or other officer authorized by law to exercise judicial power and shall be entitled to trial within a reasonable time or to release. It shall not be the general rule that persons awaiting trial shall be detained in custody, but release may be subject to guarantees to appear for trial, at any other stage of the judicial proceedings, and, should occasion arise, for execution of the judgment.

4. Anyone who is deprived of his liberty by arrest or detention shall be entitled to take proceedings before a court, in order that that court may decide without delay on the lawfulness of his detention and order his release if the detention is not lawful.

5. Anyone who has been the victim of unlawful arrest or detention shall have an enforceable right to compensation.

---

[3] One simply must ask what "normal civil obligations" and "forced labour" might have in common.

Article 10

1. All persons deprived of their liberty shall be treated with humanity and with respect for the inherent dignity of the human person.

2.
   (a) Accused persons shall, save in exceptional circumstances, be segregated from convicted persons and shall be subject to separate treatment appropriate to their status as unconvicted persons;
   (b) Accused juvenile persons shall be separated from adults and brought as speedily as possible for adjudication.

3. The penitentiary system shall comprise treatment of prisoners the essential aim of which shall be their reformation and social rehabilitation. Juvenile offenders shall be segregated from adults and be accorded treatment appropriate to their age and legal status.

Article 11

No one shall be imprisoned merely on the ground of inability to fulfill a contractual obligation.

Article 12

1. Everyone lawfully within the territory of a State shall, within that territory, have the right to liberty of movement and freedom to choose his residence.

2. Everyone shall be free to leave any country, including his own.

3. *The above-mentioned rights shall not be subject to any restrictions except those which are provided by law, are necessary to protect national security, public order (ordre public), public health or morals or the rights and freedoms of others, and are consistent with the other rights recognized in the present Covenant.*

4. No one shall be arbitrarily deprived of the right to enter his own country.

Article 13

An alien lawfully in the territory of a State Party to the present Covenant may expelled therefrom only in pursuance of a decision reached in accordance with law and shall, except where compelling reasons of national security otherwise require, be allowed to submit the reasons against his expulsion and to have his case reviewed by, and be represented for the purpose before, the competent authority or a person or persons especially designated by the competent authority.

Article 14

1. All persons shall be equal before the courts and tribunals. In the determination of any criminal charge against him, or of his rights and obligations in a suit at law, everyone shall be entitled to a fair and public hearing by a competent, independent and impartial tribunal established by law. The Press and the public may be excluded from all or part of a trial for reasons of morals, public order (ordre public) or national security in a democratic society, or when the interest of the private lives of the parties so requires, or to the extent strictly necessary in the opinion of the court in special circumstances where publicity would prejudice the interests of justice; but any judgment rendered in a criminal case or in a suit at law shall be made public except where the interest of juvenile persons otherwise requires or the proceedings concern matrimonial disputes or the guardianship of children.

2. Everyone charged with a criminal offense shall have the right to be presumed innocent until proved guilty according to law.

3. In the determination of any criminal charge against him, everyone shall be entitled to the following minimum guarantees, in full equality:
   (a) To be informed promptly and in detail in a language which he understands of the nature and cause of the charge against him;
   (b) To have adequate time and facilities for the preparation of his defense and to communicate with counsel of his own choosing;
   (c) To be tried without undue delay;

(d) To be tried in his presence, and to defend himself in person or through legal assistance of his own choosing; to be informed, if he does not have legal assistance, of this right; and to have legal assistance assigned to him, in any case where the interests of justice so require, and without payment by him in any such case if he does not have sufficient means to pay for it;

(e) To examine, or have examined, the witnesses against him and to obtain the attendance and examination of witnesses on his behalf under the same conditions as witnesses against him;

(f) To have the free assistance of an interpreter if he cannot understand or speak the language used in court;

(g) Not to be compelled to testify against himself or to confess guilt.

4. In the case of juvenile persons, the procedure shall be such as will take account of their age and the desirability of promoting their rehabilitation.

5. Everyone convicted of a crime shall have the right to his conviction and sentence being reviewed by a higher tribunal according to law.

6. When a person has by a final decision been convicted of a criminal offense and when subsequently his conviction has been reversed or he has been pardoned on the ground that a new or newly discovered fact shows conclusively that there has been a miscarriage of justice, the person who has suffered punishment as a result of such conviction shall be compensated according to law, unless it is proved that the non-disclosure of the unknown fact in time is wholly or partly attributable to him.

7. No one shall be liable to be tried or punished again for an offense for which he has already been finally convicted or acquitted in accordance with the law and penal procedure of each country.

Article 15

No one shall be held guilty of any criminal offense on account of any act or omission which did not constitute a criminal offense, under national or international law, at the time when it was committed.

Nor shall a heavier penalty be imposed than the one that was applicable at the time when the criminal offense was committed. If, subsequent to the commission of the offense, provision is made by law for the imposition of a lighter penalty, the offender shall benefit thereby.

Nothing in this article shall prejudice the trial and punishment of any person for any act or omission which, at the time when it was committed, was criminal according to the general principles of law recognized by the community of nations.[5]

Article 16

Everyone shall have the right to recognition everywhere as a person before the law.

Article 17

1. No one shall be subjected to arbitrary or unlawful interference with his privacy, family, home or correspondence, nor to unlawful attacks on his honour and reputation.

2. Everyone has the right to the protection of the law against such interference or attacks.

Article 18

1. Everyone shall have the right to freedom of thought, conscience and religion. This right shall include freedom to have or to adopt a religion or belief of his choice, and freedom, either individually or in community with others and in public or private, to manifest his religion or belief in worship, observance, practice and teaching.

2. No one shall be subject to coercion which would impair his freedom to have or to adopt a religion or belief of his choice.

3. *Freedom to manifest one's religion or beliefs may be subject only to such limitations as are prescribed by law and are necessary to protect public*

[5] But, please reread the previous paragraph.

safety, order, health, or morals or the fundamental rights and freedoms of others.

4. The States Parties to the present Covenant undertake to have respect for the liberty of parents and, when applicable, legal guardians to ensure the religious and moral education of their children in conformity with their own convictions.

Article 19

1. Everyone shall have the right to hold opinions without interference.

2. Everyone shall have the right to freedom of expression; this right shall include freedom to seek, receive and impart information and ideas of all kinds, regardless of frontiers, either orally, in writing or in print, in the form of art, or through any other media of his choice.

3. The exercise of the rights provided for in paragraph 2 of this article carries with it special duties and responsibilities. *It may therefore be subject to certain restrictions, but these shall only be such as are provided by law and are necessary:*[6]
   (a) For respect of the rights or reputations of others;
   (b) For the protection of national security or of public order (ordre public), or of public health or morals.

Article 20

1. Any propaganda for war shall be prohibited by law.

2. Any advocacy of national, racial or religious hatred that constitutes incitement to discrimination, hostility or violence shall be prohibited by law.

Article 21

The right of peaceful assembly shall be recognized. *No restrictions may be placed on the exercise of this right other than those imposed in con-*

---

[6] I swear I am not making this up.

formity with the law and which are necessary in a democratic society in the interests of national security or public safety, public order (ordre public), the protection of public health or morals or the protection of the rights and freedoms of others.

Article 22

1. Everyone shall have the right to freedom of association with others, including the right to form and join trade unions for the protection of his interests.

2. *No restrictions may be placed on the exercise of this right other than those which are prescribed by law and which are necessary in a democratic society in the interests of national security or public safety, public order (ordre public), the protection of public health or morals or the protection of the rights and freedoms of others.* This article shall not prevent the imposition of lawful restrictions on members of the armed forces and of the police in their exercise of this right.

3. Nothing in this article shall authorize States Parties to the International Labour Organization Convention of 1948 concerning Freedom of Association and Protection of the Right to Organize to take legislative measures which would prejudice, or to apply the law in such a manner as to prejudice, the guarantees provided for in that Convention.

Article 23

1. The family is the natural and fundamental group unit of society and is entitled to protection by society and the State.

2. The right of men and women of marriageable age to marry and to found a family shall be recognized.

3. No marriage shall be entered into without the free and full consent of the intending spouses.

4. States Parties to the present Covenant shall take appropriate steps to ensure equally of rights and responsibilities of spouses as to mar-

riage, *during marriage* and at its dissolution. In the case of dissolution, provision shall be made for the necessary protection of any children.

Article 24

1. Every child shall have, without any discrimination as to race, colour, sex, language, religion, national or social origin, property or birth, the right to such measures of protection as are required by his status as a minor, on the part of his family, society and the State.

2. *Every child shall be registered immediately after birth and shall have a name.*

3. Every child has the right to acquire a nationality.

Article 25

Every citizen shall have the right and the opportunity, without any of the distinctions mentioned in article 2 and without unreasonable restrictions:

- (a) To take part in the conduct of public affairs, directly or through freely chosen representatives;
- (b) To vote and to be elected at genuine periodic elections which shall be by universal and equal suffrage and shall be held by secret ballot, guaranteeing the free expression of the will of the electors;
- (c) To have access, on general terms of equality, to public service in his country.

Article 26

All persons are equal before the law and are entitled without any discrimination to the equal protection of the law. In this respect, the law shall prohibit any discrimination and guarantee to all persons equal and effective protection against discrimination on any ground such as race, colour, sex, language, religion, political or other opinion, national or social origin, property, birth or other status.

Article 27

In those States in which ethnic, religious or linguistic minorities
exist, persons belonging to such minorities shall not be denied the
right, in community with the other members of their group, to enjoy
their own culture, to profess and practice their own religion, or to use
their own language.

[The balance of this document, roughly 50 percent more, establishes the bureaucratic structures appropriate for review and enforcement of these so-called rights.]

The complete text may be found at many locations on the Web including:
http://www.unhchr.ch/html/menu3/b/a_ccpr.htm

International Covenant on Economic, Social and Cultural Rights

Adopted and opened for signature, ratification and accession by General Assembly resolution 2200A (XXI) of 16 December 1966. Entry into force 3 January 1976, in accordance with article 27

Preamble

The States Parties to the Present Covenant,

CONSIDERING that, in accordance with the principles proclaimed in the Charter of the United Nations, recognition of the inherent dignity and of the equal and inalienable rights of all members of the human family is the foundation of freedom, justice and peace in the world,

RECOGNIZING that these rights derive from the inherent dignity of the human person,

RECOGNIZING that, in accordance with the Universal Declaration of Human Rights, the ideal of free human beings enjoying freedom from fear and want can only be achieved if conditions are created whereby everyone may enjoy his economic, social and cultural rights, as well as his civil and political rights,

CONSIDERING the obligation of States under the Charter of the United Nations to promote universal respect for, and observance of, human rights and freedoms,

REALIZING that the individual, having duties to other individuals and the community to which he belongs, is under a responsibility to strive for the promotion and observance of the rights recognized in the present Covenant,

AGREE upon the following articles:

PART I

Article 1

(1) All peoples have the right of self-determination. By virtue of that right they freely determine their political status and freely pursue their economic, social and cultural development.

(2) All people may, for their own ends, freely dispose of their natural wealth and resources without prejudice to any obligations arising out of international economic co-operation, based upon the principle of mutual benefit, and international law. In no case may a people be deprived of its own means of subsistence.

(3) The States Parties to the present Covenant, including those having responsibility for the administration of Non-Self-Governing and Trust Territories, shall promote the realization of the right to self-determination, and shall respect that right, in conformity with the provisions of the Charter of the United Nations.

PART II

Article 2

(1) Each State Party to the present Covenant undertakes to take steps, individually and through international assistance and cooperation, especially economic and technical, to the maximum of its available resources, with a view to achieving progressively the full realization of the rights recognized in the present Covenant by all appropriate means, including in particular the adoption of legislative measures.

(2) The States Parties to the present Covenant undertake to guarantee that the rights enunciated in the present Covenant will be exercised without discrimination of any kind as to race, colour, sex, language, religion, political or other opinion, national or social origin, property, birth or other status.

(3) Developing countries, with due regard to human rights and their national economy, may determine to what extent they would guarantee the economic rights recognized in the present Covenant to non-nationals.

Article 3

The States Parties to the present Covenant undertake to ensure the equal right of men and women to the enjoyment of all economic, social and cultural rights set forth in the present Covenant.

Article 4

The States Parties to the present Covenant recognize that, in the enjoyment of those rights provided by the State in conformity with the present Covenant, *the State may subject such rights only to such limitations as are determined by law only in so far as this may be compatible with the nature of these rights and solely for the purpose of promoting the general welfare in a democratic society.*

Article 5

(1) Nothing in the present Covenant may be interpreted as implying for any State, group or person any right to engage in any activity or to perform any act aimed at the destruction of any of the rights and freedoms recognized herein, or at their limitation to a greater extent than is provided for in the present Covenant.

(2) No restriction upon or derogation from any of the fundamental human rights recognized or existing in any country in virtue of law, conventions, regulations or custom shall be admitted on the pretext that the present Covenant does not recognize such rights or that it recognizes them to a lesser extent.

PART III

Article 6

(1) The States Parties to the present Covenant recognize *the right to work*, which includes the right of everyone to the opportunity to gain his living by work which he freely chooses or accepts, and will take appropriate steps to safeguard this right.

(2) The steps to be taken by a State Party to the present Covenant to achieve the full realization of this right shall include *technical and vocational guidance and training programmes, policies and techniques to achieve steady economic, social and cultural development and full and productive employment under conditions safe-guarding fundamental political and economic freedoms to the individual.*

Article 7

The States Parties to the present Covenant recognize the right of everyone to the enjoyment of just and favourable conditions of work which ensure, in particular:

(a) Remuneration which provides all workers, as a minimum, with:
   (i) *Fair wages and equal remuneration for work of equal value* without distinction of any kind, in particular women being guaranteed conditions of work not inferior to those enjoyed by men, with equal pay for equal work;
   (ii) A *decent living* for themselves and their families in accordance with the provisions of the present Covenant;[1]
(b) Safe and healthy working conditions;
(c) Equal opportunity for everyone to be promoted in his employment to an appropriate higher level, subject to no considerations other than those of seniority and competence;
(d) Rest, leisure and reasonable limitation of working hours and *periodic holidays with pay*, as well as *remuneration for public holidays.*[2]

---

[1] "Fair" wages, and a "decent" living are so arbitrary as to be meaningless. By what precise criteria will these be enforced? When words have no meaning, life becomes dangerous. Please reread Orwell's *1984*.
[2] I'll bet UN Day would be a paid holiday.

Article 8

(1) The States Parties to the present Covenant undertake to ensure:

(a) The right of everyone to form trade unions and join the trade union of his choice, subject only to the rules of the organization concerned, for the promotion and protection of his economic and social interests. *No restrictions may be placed on the exercise of this right other than those prescribed by law and which are necessary in a democratic society in the interests of national security or public order or for the protection of the rights and freedoms of others;*

(b) The right of trade unions to establish national federations or confederations and the right of the latter to form or join international trade-union organizations;

(c) The right of trade unions to function freely *subject to no limitations other than those prescribed by law and which are necessary in a democratic society in the interests of national security or public order or for the protection of the rights and freedoms of others;*

(d) The right to strike, provided that it is exercised in conformity with the laws of the particular country.

(2) This article shall not prevent the imposition of lawful restrictions on the exercise of these rights by members of the armed forces or of the police or of the administration of the State.

(3) Nothing in this article shall authorize States Parties to the International Labour Organization Convention of 1948 concerning Freedom of Association and Protection of the Right to Organize to take legislative measures which would prejudice, or apply the law in such a manner as would prejudice, the guarantees provided for in that Convention.

Article 9

The States Parties to the present Covenant recognize the *right of everyone to social security, including social insurance*.

Article 10

The States Parties to the present Covenant recognize that:

(1) The widest possible protection and assistance should be accorded to the family, which is the natural and fundamental group unit of society, particularly for its establishment and while it is responsible for the care and education of dependent children. Marriage must be entered into with the free consent of the intending spouses.

(2) Special protection should be accorded to mothers during a reasonable period before and after childbirth. During such period working mothers should be accorded paid leave or leave with adequate social security benefits.

(3) Special measures of protection and assistance should be taken on behalf of all children and young persons without discrimination for reasons of parentage or other conditions. Children and young persons should be protected from economic and social exploitation. Their employment in work harmful to their morals or health or dangerous to life or likely to hamper their normal development should be punishable by law. States should also set age limits below which the paid employment of child labour should be prohibited and punishable by law.

Article 11

(1) The States Parties to the present Covenant recognize *the right of everyone to an adequate standard of living for himself and his family, including adequate food, clothing and housing, and to the continuous improvement of living conditions.* The States Parties will take appropriate steps to ensure the realization of this right, recognizing to this effect the essential importance of international cooperation based on free consent.

(2) The States Parties to the present Covenant, recognizing *the fundamental right of everyone to be free from hunger,* shall take, individually and through international co-operation, the measures, including specific programmes, which are needed:

(a) To improve methods of production, conservation and distribution of food by making full use of technical and scientific knowledge, by disseminating knowledge of the principles of nutrition and by developing or reforming agrarian systems in such a way as to achieve the most efficient development and utilization of natural resources;

(b) Taking into account the problems of both food-importing and food- exporting countries, *to ensure the equitable distribution of world food supplies in relation to need.*

Article 12

(1) The States Parties to the present Covenant recognize *the right of everyone to the enjoyment of the highest attainable standard of physical and mental health.*

(2) The steps to be taken by the States Parties to the present Covenant to achieve the full realization of this right shall include those necessary for:

(a) The provision for the reduction of the stillbirth-rate and of infant mortality and for the healthy development of the child;

(b) The improvement of all aspects of environmental and industrial hygiene;

(c) The prevention, treatment and control of epidemic, endemic, occupational and other diseases;

(d) *The creation of conditions which would assure to all medical service and medical attention in the event of sickness.*

Article 13

(1) The States Parties to the present Covenant recognize *the right of everyone to education.* They agree that education shall be directed to the full development of the human personality and the sense of its dignity, and shall strengthen the respect for human rights and fundamental freedoms. They further agree that education shall enable all persons to participate effectively in a free society, promote understanding, tolerance and friendship among all nations and all racial, ethnic or religious groups, *and further the activities of the United Nations for the maintenance of peace.*

(2) The States Parties to the present Covenant recognize that, with a view to achieving the full realization of this right:

    (a) *Primary education shall be compulsory and available free to all;*[3]

    (b) Secondary education in its different forms, including technical and vocational secondary education, shall be made generally available and accessible to all by every appropriate means, and in particular by the *progressive introduction of free education;*

    (c) Higher education shall be make equally accessible to all, on the basis of capacity, by every appropriate means, and in particular by the *progressive introduction of free education;*

    (d) Fundamental education shall be encouraged or intensified as far as possible for those persons who have not received or completed the whole period of their primary education;

    (e) The development of a system of schools at all levels shall be actively pursued, an adequate fellowship system shall be established, and the material conditions of teaching staff shall be continuously improved.

(3) The States Parties to the present Covenant undertake to have respect for the liberty of parents and, when applicable, legal guardians to choose for their children schools, other than those established by the public authorities, which conform to such minimum educational standards as may be laid down or approved by the State and *to ensure the religious and moral education of their children in conformity with their own convictions.*[4]

(4) No part of this article shall be construed so as to interfere with the liberty of individuals and bodies to establish and direct educational institutions, *subject always to the observance of the principles set forth in paragraph 1 of this article* and to the requirement that the education given in such institutions shall conform to such minimum standards as may be laid down by the State.[5]

---

[3] Not only is it a "right" (see paragraph 1 of article 13), it is a compulsory right. As far as education being "free," (see also b and c) one can almost hear Butthead telling Beavis, "Free stuff is cool." As an adult, I'm forced to ask, "Who pays for the free stuff?"

[4] Wonder if this would allow home schooling? See especially following paragraph.

[5] Unless, of course, the convictions of the parents mentioned in preceding paragraph conflict with the "activities of the United Nations" mentioned in paragraph 1 of article 13.

Article 14

Each State Party to the present Covenant which, at the time of becoming a Party, has not been able to secure in its metropolitan territory or other territories under its jurisdiction compulsory primary education, free of charge, undertakes, within two years, to work out and adopt a detailed plan of action for the progressive implementation, within a reasonable number of years, to be fixed in the plan, of the principle of compulsory education free of charge for all.

Article 15

(1) The States Parties to the present Covenant recognize the right of everyone:
   (a) To take part in cultural life;
   (b) To enjoy the benefits of scientific progress and its applications;
   (c) To benefit from the protection of the moral and material interests resulting from any scientific, literary or artistic production of which he is the author.

(2) The steps to be taken by the States Parties to the present Covenant to achieve the full realization of this right shall include those necessary for the conservation, the development and diffusion of science and culture.

(3) The States Parties to the present Covenant undertake to respect the freedom indispensable for scientific research and creative activity.

(4) The States Parties to the present Covenant recognize the benefits to be derived from the encouragement and development of international contacts and co-operation in the scientific and cultural fields.

[The balance of this document, roughly 30 percent more, establishes the bureaucratic structures appropriate for review and enforcement of these so-called rights.]

The complete text may be found at many locations on the Web including:
http://193.194.138.190/html/menu3/b/a_cescr.htm

INTERNATIONAL CONVENTION ON THE ELIMINATION OF ALL FORMS OF RACIAL DISCRIMINATION

Adopted and opened for signature and ratification by General Assembly resolution 2106 (XX) of 21 December 1965. Entry into force 4 January 1969, in accordance with Article 19

The States Parties to this Convention,

CONSIDERING that the Charter of the United Nations is based on the principles of the dignity and equality inherent in all human beings, and that all Member States have pledged themselves to take joint and separate action, in co-operation with the Organization, for the achievement of one of the purposes of the United Nations which is to promote and encourage universal respect for and observance of human rights and fundamental freedoms for all, without distinction as to race, sex, language or religion,

CONSIDERING that the Universal Declaration of Human Rights proclaims that all human beings are born free and equal in dignity and rights and that everyone is entitled to all the rights and freedoms set out therein, without distinction of any kind, in particular as to race, colour or national origin,

CONSIDERING that all human beings are equal before the law and are entitled to equal protection of the law against any discrimination and against any incitement to discrimination,

CONSIDERING that the United Nations has condemned colonialism and all practices of segregation and discrimination associated therewith, in whatever form and wherever they exist, and that the Declaration on the Granting of Independence to Colonial Countries and Peoples of 14 December 1960 (General Assembly resolution 1514 (XV)) has affirmed and solemnly proclaimed the necessity of bringing them to a speedy and unconditional end,

CONSIDERING that the United Nations Declaration on the Elimination of All Forms of Racial Discrimination of 20 November 1963 (General Assembly resolution 1904 (XVIII)) solemnly affirms the necessity of speedily eliminating racial discrimination throughout the world in all its forms and manifestations and of securing under-standing of and respect for the dignity of the human person,

CONVINCED that any doctrine of superiority based on racial differen-tiation is scientifically false, morally condemnable, socially unjust and dangerous, and that there is no justification for racial discrimi-nation, in theory or in practice, anywhere,

REAFFIRMING that discrimination between human beings on the grounds of race, colour or ethnic origin is an obstacle to friendly and peaceful relations among nations and is capable of disturbing peace and security among peoples and the harmony of persons living side by side even within one and the same State,

CONVINCED that the existence of racial barriers is repugnant to the ideals of any human society,

ALARMED by manifestations of racial discrimination still in evidence in some areas of the world and by governmental policies based on racial superiority or hatred, such as policies of apartheid, segregation or separation,

RESOLVED to adopt all necessary measures for speedily eliminating racial discrimination in all its forms and manifestations, and to pre-vent and combat racist doctrines and practices in order to promote understanding between races and to build an international commu-nity free from all forms of racial segregation and racial discrimina-tion,

BEARING IN MIND the Convention concerning Discrimination in respect of Employment and Occupation adopted by the Internation-al Labour Organisation in 1958, and the Convention against Dis-crimination in Education adopted by the United Nations Educational, Scientific and Cultural Organization in 1960,

DESIRING to implement the principles embodied in the United Nations Declaration on the Elimination of Al l Forms of Racial Dis-crimination and to secure the earliest adoption of practical measures to that end,

HAVE AGREED as follows:

PART I

Article 1

1. In this Convention, the term "racial discrimination" shall mean any *distinction, exclusion, restriction or preference* based on race, colour, descent, or national or ethnic origin which has the purpose or effect of nullifying or impairing the recognition, enjoyment or exercise, on an equal footing, of human rights and fundamental freedoms in the political, economic, social, cultural or any other field of public life.[1]

2. This Convention shall not apply to distinctions, exclusions, restrictions or preferences made by a State Party to this Convention between citizens and non-citizens.

3. Nothing in this Convention may be interpreted as affecting in any way the legal provisions of States Parties concerning nationality, citizenship or naturalization, provided that such provisions do not discriminate against any particular nationality.

4. *Special measures taken for the sole purpose of securing adequate advancement of certain racial or ethnic groups or individuals* requiring such protection as may be necessary in order to ensure such groups or individuals equal enjoyment or exercise of human rights and fundamental freedoms *shall not be deemed racial discrimination*, provided, however, that such measures do not, as a consequence, lead to the maintenance of separate rights for different racial groups and that they shall not be continued after the objectives for which they were taken have been achieved.[2]

Article 2

1. States Parties *condemn racial discrimination* and undertake to pursue by all appropriate means and without delay *a policy of eliminating racial discrimination in all its forms* and promoting understanding among all races, and, to this end:[3]

---

[1] However, please see Paragraph 4.
[2] In other words, "approved" racial discrimination against certain groups shall not be considered "bad" racial discrimination against other groups.
[3] However, please see paragraph 2 below.

(a) Each State Party undertakes to engage in no act or practice of racial discrimination against persons, groups of persons or institutions and to ensure that all public authorities and public institutions, national and local, shall act in conformity with this obligation;

(b) Each State Party undertakes not to sponsor, defend or support racial discrimination by any persons or organizations;

(c) Each State Party shall take effective measures to review governmental, national and local policies, and to amend, rescind or nullify any laws and regulations which have the effect of creating or perpetuating racial discrimination wherever it exists;

(d) Each State Party shall prohibit and bring to an end, by all appropriate means, including legislation as required by circumstances, racial discrimination by any persons, group or organization;

(e) Each State Party undertakes to encourage, where appropriate, integrationist multiracial organizations and movements and other means of eliminating barriers between races, and to discourage anything which tends to strengthen racial division.

2. *States Parties shall,* when the circumstances so warrant, *take,* in the social, economic, cultural and other fields, *special and concrete measures to ensure the adequate development and protection of certain racial groups or individuals* belonging to them, for the purpose of guaranteeing them the full and equal enjoyment of human rights and fundamental freedoms. These measures shall in no case entail as a consequence the maintenance of unequal or separate rights for different racial groups after the objectives for which they were taken have been achieved.

Article 3

States Parties particularly condemn racial segregation and apartheid and undertake to prevent, prohibit and eradicate all practices of this nature in territories under their jurisdiction.

Article 4

States Parties condemn all propaganda and all organizations which are based on ideas or theories of superiority of one race or group of persons of one colour or ethnic origin, or which attempt to justify or promote racial hatred and discrimination in any form, and undertake to adopt immediate and positive measures designed to eradicate all incitement to, or acts of, such discrimination and, to this end, with due regard to the principles embodied in the Universal Declaration of Human Rights and the rights expressly set forth in article 5 of this Convention, inter alia:

(a) *Shall declare an offense punishable by law all dissemination of ideas based on racial superiority or hatred, incitement to racial discrimination,* as well as all acts of violence or incitement to such acts against any race or group of persons of another colour or ethnic origin, *and also the provision of any assistance to racist activities, including the financing thereof;*[4]

(b) *Shall declare illegal and prohibit organizations, and also organized and all other propaganda activities,* which promote and incite racial discrimination, and shall recognize *participation in such organizations or activities as an offense punishable by law;*[5]

(c) Shall not permit public authorities or public institutions, national or local, to promote or incite racial discrimination.

Article 5

In compliance with the fundamental obligations laid down in article 2 of this Convention, States Parties undertake to prohibit and to eliminate racial discrimination in all its forms and to guarantee the right of everyone, without distinction as to race, colour, or national or ethnic origin, to equality before the law, notably in the enjoyment of the following rights

(a) The right to equal treatment before the tribunals and all other organs administering justice;

---

[4] See Declaration of Human Rights Article 19.
[5] See Declaration of Human Rights Article 20.

(b) The right to security of person and protection by the State against violence or bodily harm, whether inflicted by government officials or by any individual group or institution;

(c) Political rights, in particular the right to participate in elections — to vote and to stand for election — on the basis of universal and equal suffrage, to take part in the Government as well as in the conduct of public affairs at any level and to have equal access to public service;

(d) Other civil rights, in particular:
   (i) The right to freedom of movement and residence within the border of the State;
   (ii) The right to leave any country, including one's own, and to return to one's country;
   (iii) The right to nationality;
   (iv) The right to marriage and choice of spouse;
   (v) The right to own property alone as well as in association with others;
   (vi) The right to inherit;
   (vii) The right to *freedom of thought, conscience and religion;*[6]
   (viii) The right to *freedom of opinion and expression;*[7]
   (ix) The right to *freedom of peaceful assembly and association;*[8]

(e) Economic, social and cultural rights, in particular:
   (i) The rights to work, to *free choice of employment*, to just and favourable conditions of work, to protection against unemployment, to equal pay for equal work, to *just and favourable remuneration;*
   (ii) The right to form and join trade unions;
   (iii) The *right to housing;*
   (iv) The *right to public health, medical care, social security and social services;*
   (v) The *right to education and training;*
   (vi) The *right to equal participation in cultural activities;*[9]

---

[6] More properly "approved" thought, etc. See article 4.
[7] More properly "approved" opinion, etc. See article 4.
[8] More properly "approved" association, etc. See article 4.
[9] Does this mean an untalented musician be free to join the orchestra of his or her choice?

(f) The right of access to any place or service intended for use by the general public, such as transport hotels, restaurants, cafes, theatres and parks.

Article 6

States Parties shall assure to everyone within their jurisdiction effective protection and remedies, through the competent national tribunals and other State institutions, against any acts of racial discrimination which violate his human rights and fundamental freedoms contrary to this Convention, as well as the *right to seek from such tribunals just and adequate reparation* or satisfaction for any damage suffered as a result of such discrimination.[10]

Article 7

States Parties undertake to adopt immediate and effective measures, particularly in the fields of teaching, education, culture and information, with a view to combating prejudices which lead to racial discrimination and to promoting understanding, tolerance and friendship among nations and racial or ethnical groups, *as well as to propagating the purposes and principles of the Charter of the United Nations, the Universal Declaration of Human Rights, the United Nations Declaration on the Elimination of All Forms of Racial Discrimination, and this Convention.*

---

[10] Interestingly enough, an article posted on WorldNetDaily on August 22, 2003 discussed a reparations lawsuit being mounted by Egyptians against Jews. The suit claims reparations for gold, furniture, kitchen utensils, clothing, etc. said to be stolen by Jewish slaves during the Exodus some 5,758 years ago. This is truly the Mother of all reparations lawsuits!
http://www.worldnetdaily.com/news/article.asp?ARTICLE_ID=34227

[The balance of this document, just over 50 percent more, establishes the bureaucratic structures appropriate for review and enforcement of these so-called rights.]

The complete text may be found at many locations on the Web including:
http://www.unhchr.ch/html/menu3/b/d_icerd.htm

The Language of Treason

The following travesty was personally presented to the UN by President John F. Kennedy on September 25, 1961. It is as an official expression of U.S. policy. It has never been rescinded by succeeding administrations.

More than any other argument advanced in this book, *Freedom From War* provides irrefutable evidence that people within the American government are seeking to subvert the Constitution and surrender American sovereignty to a world government. *Freedom From War* is the smoking gun.

One may disagree that world government is undesirable. One may believe that international control of nuclear arsenals, and the other sophisticated weapons of war, could make the world a safer place to live.

But, after reading the following, one may no longer disagree that the goal of those who support our continued involvement in the UN is the building of a framework for eventual American submergence under a world government.

There is a peculiar personal irony here. After my wake-up call to the problem of tyranny in America in 1992, I begin to investigate the Kennedy assassination. I was 15 when he was killed. I remember admiring his vigor, and participated enthusiastically in the physical fitness program he promoted for young people. The Peace Corp resonated with my adolescent idealism. What a welcome change from Eisenhower. Like many Americans, I was devastated by his murder. I held a fond regard for him throughout my life. I viewed his death and the Vietnam War as the two most significant contributing factors to the undermining of my generation's patriotism.

I never bothered with the details of his assassination, nor worried about it being a particular mystery. I accepted the official conclusions with little interest. Of course there were always rumors of conspiracy, but I paid scant attention. His death was a painful wound I never cared to reopen. After the Weaver incident, however, I plunged into the Kennedy case in great detail. It was my first hard look behind the veil.

Imagine my surprise when I came across *Freedom From War* at the conclusion of that research!

John F. Kennedy violated his oath to uphold the American way of life as proclaimed by America's Founding Fathers in the words reproduced in appendix one.

Note how the language of *Freedom From War* mimics that of the UN documents reproduced in appendix two.

I am going to make an uncharacteristically tolerant comment about President Kennedy and his ilk.

It is always hard for a person to put himself in the mindset of another. I did not experience World War II. Kennedy did. Perhaps, he was manipulated by a combination of factors that might have included his own experience of the horrors of war, his idealism, the mental confusion caused by his drug addiction, and his political ambitions.

I have no way of knowing whether he was a willing traitor, or merely a dupe of more intelligent and sinister forces. However, since U.S. presidents and policy makers who followed him (both "liberal" and "conservative," Demican and Republicrat), have never officially repudiated *Freedom From War*, Kennedy's personal motives are, frankly, irrelevant.

Please note that all typographic styling, such as the use of italics and boldface type, is as the original. I make no editorial comment within the text of *Freedom From War* beyond faithful reproduction.

FREEDOM FROM WAR

THE UNITED STATES PROGRAM FOR GENERAL AND COMPLETE DISARMAMENT IN A PEACEFUL WORLD

Introduction

The revolutionary development of modern weapons within a world divided by serious ideological differences has produced a crisis in human history. In order to overcome the danger of nuclear war now confronting mankind, the United States has introduced at the Sixteenth General Assembly of the United Nations a *Program for General and Complete Disarmament in a Peaceful World*.

This new program provides for the progressive reduction of the war-making capabilities of nations and the simultaneous strengthening of international institutions to settle disputes and maintain the peace. It sets forth a series of comprehensive measures which can and should be taken in order to bring about a world in which there will be freedom from war and security for all states. It is based on three principles deemed essential to the achievement of practical progress in the disarmament field:

First, there must be immediate disarmament action:

A strenuous and uninterrupted effort must be made toward the goal of general and complete disarmament; at the same time, it is important that specific measures be put into effect as soon as possible.

Second, all disarmament obligations must be subject to effective international controls:

The control organizations must have the manpower, facilities, and effectiveness to assure that limitations or reductions take place as agreed. It must also be able to certify to all states that retained forces and armaments do not exceed those permitted at any stage of the disarmament process.

Third, adequate peace-keeping machinery must be established:

There is an inseparable relationship between the scaling down of national armaments on the one hand and the building up of international peace-keeping machinery and institutions on the other. Nations are unlikely to shed their means of self-protection in the absence of alternative ways to safeguard their legitimate interests. This can only be achieved through the progressive strengthening of international institutions under the United Nations and by creating a United Nations Peace Force to enforce the peace as the disarmament process proceeds.

There follows a summary of the principal provisions of the United States *Program for General and Complete Disarmament in a Peaceful World*. The full text of the program is contained in an appendix to this pamphlet.

Freedom From War

The United States Program For General And Complete Disarmament In A Peaceful World

Summary

Disarmament Goal and Objectives

The over-all goal of the United States is a free, secure, and peaceful world of independent states adhering to common standards of justice and international conduct and subjecting the use of force to the rule of law; a world which has achieved general and complete disarmament under effective international control; and a world in which adjustment to change takes place in accordance with the principles of the United Nations.

In order to make possible the achievement of that goal, the program sets forth the following specific objectives toward which nations should direct their efforts:

- The disbanding of all national armed forces and the prohibition of their reestablishment in any form whatsoever other than those required to preserve internal order and for contributions to a United Nations Peace Force;
- The elimination from national arsenals of all armaments, including all weapons of mass destruction and the means for their delivery, other than those required for a United Nations Peace Force and for maintaining internal order;
- The institution of effective means for the enforcement of international agreements, for the settlement of disputes, and for the maintenance of peace in accordance with the principles of the United Nations;
- The establishment and effective operation of an International Disarmament Organization within the framework of the United Nations to insure compliance at all times with all disarmament obligations.

Task of Negotiating States

The negotiating states are called upon to develop the program into a detailed plan for general and complete disarmament and to continue their efforts without interruption until the whole program has been achieved. To this end, they are to seek the widest possible area of agreement at the earliest possible date. At the same time, and without prejudice to progress on the disarmament program, they are to seek agreement on those immediate measures that would contribute to the common security of nations and that could facilitate and form part of the total program.

Governing Principles

The program sets forth a series of general principles to guide the negotiating states in their work. These make clear that:

- As states relinquish their arms, the United Nations must be progressively strengthened in order to improve its capacity to assure international security and the peaceful settlement of disputes;
- Disarmament must proceed as rapidly as possible, until it is completed, in stages containing balanced, phased, and safeguarded measures;
- Each measure and stage should be carried out in an agreed period of time, with transition from one stage to the next to take place as soon as all measures in the preceding stage have been carried out and verified and as soon as necessary arrangements for verification of the next stage have been made;
- Inspection and verification must establish both that nations carry out scheduled limitations or reductions and that they do not retain armed forces and armaments in excess of those permitted at any stage of the disarmament process; and
- Disarmament must take place in a manner that will not affect adversely the security of any state.

Disarmament Stages

The program provides for progressive disarmament steps to take place in three stages and for the simultaneous strengthening of international institutions.

First Stage

The first stage contains measures which would significantly reduce the capabilities of nations to wage aggressive war. Implementation of this stage would mean that:

- **The nuclear threat would be reduced:**

All states would have adhered to a treaty effectively prohibiting the testing of nuclear weapons.

The production of fissionable materials for use in weapons would be stopped and quantities of such materials from past production would be converted to non-weapons uses.

States owning nuclear weapons would not relinquish control of such weapons to any nation not owning them and would not transmit to any such nation information or material necessary for their manufacture.

States not owning nuclear weapons would not manufacture them or attempt to obtain control of such weapons belonging to other states.

A Commission of Experts would be established to report on the feasibility and means for the verified reduction and eventual elimination of nuclear weapons stockpiles.

- **Strategic delivery vehicles would be reduced:**

Strategic nuclear weapons delivery vehicles of specified categories and weapons designed to counter such vehicles would be reduced to agreed levels by equitable and balanced steps; their production would be discontinued or limited; their testing would be limited or halted.

- **Arms and armed forces would be reduced:**

The armed forces of the United States and the Soviet Union would be limited to 2.1 million men each (with appropriate levels not exceeding that amount for other militarily significant states); levels of armaments would be correspondingly reduced and their production would be limited.

An Experts Commission would be established to examine and

report on the feasibility and means of accomplishing verifiable reduction and eventual elimination of all chemical, biological and radiological weapons.

- **Peaceful use of outer space would be promoted:**

The placing in orbit or stationing in outer space of weapons capable of producing mass destruction would be prohibited.

States would give advance notification of space vehicle and missile launchings.

- **U.N. peace-keeping powers would be strengthened:**

Measures would be taken to develop and strengthen United Nations arrangements for arbitration, for the development of international law, and for the establishment in Stage II of a permanent U.N. Peace Force.

- **An International Disarmament Organization would be established for effective verification of the disarmament program:**

Its functions would be expanded progressively as disarmament proceeds.

It would certify to all states that agreed reductions have taken place and that retained forces and armaments do not exceed permitted levels.

It would determine the transition from one stage to the next.

- **States would be committed to other measures to reduce international tension and to protect against the chance of war by accident, miscalculation, or surprise attack:**

States would be committed to refrain from the threat or use of any type of armed force contrary to the principles of the U.N. Charter and to refrain from indirect aggression and subversion against any country.

A U.N. peace observation group would be available to investigate any situation which might constitute a threat to or breach of the peace.

States would be committed to give advance notice of major military movements which might cause alarm; observation posts would be established to report on concentrations and movements of military forces.

Second Stage

The second stage contains a series of measures which would bring within sight a world in which there would be freedom from war. Implementation of all measures in the second stage would mean:

- Further substantial reductions in the armed forces, armaments, and military establishments of states, including strategic nuclear weapons delivery vehicles and countering weapons;
- Further development of methods for the peaceful settlement of disputes under the United Nations;
- Establishment of a permanent international peace force within the United Nations;
- Depending on the findings of an Experts Commission, a halt in the production of chemical, bacteriological, and radiological weapons and a reduction of existing stocks or their conversion to peaceful uses;
- On the basis of the findings of an Experts Commission, a reduction of stocks of nuclear weapons;
- The dismantling or the conversion to peaceful uses of certain military bases and facilities wherever located; and
- The strengthening and enlargement of the International Disarmament Organization to enable it to verify the steps taken in Stage II and to determine the transition to Stage III.

Third Stage

During the third stage of the program, the states of the world, building on the experience and confidence gained in successfully implementing the measures of the first two stages, would take final steps toward the goal of a world in which:

- States would retain only those forces, non-nuclear armaments, and establishments required for the purpose of maintaining internal order; they would also support and provide agreed man-power for a U.N. Peace Force.

- The U.N. Peace Force, equipped with agreed types and quantities of armaments, would be fully functioning.
- The manufacture of armaments would be prohibited except for those of agreed types and quantities to be used by the U.N. Peace Force and those required to maintain internal order. All other armaments would be destroyed or converted to peaceful purposes.
- The peace-keeping capabilities of the United Nations would be sufficiently strong and the obligations of all states under such arrangements sufficiently far-reaching as to assure peace and the just settlement of differences in a disarmed world.

APPENDIX

DECLARATION ON DISARMAMENT

THE UNITED STATES PROGRAM FOR GENERAL AND COMPLETE DISARMAMENT IN A PEACEFUL WORLD

The Nations of the world,

Conscious of the crisis in human history produced by the revolutionary development of modern weapons within a world divided by serious ideological differences;

Determined to save present and succeeding generations from the scourge of war and the dangers and burdens of the arms race and to create conditions in which all peoples can strive freely and peacefully to fulfill their basic aspirations;

Declare their goal to be: A free, secure, and peaceful world of independent states adhering to common standards of justice and international conduct and subjecting the use of force to the rule of law; a world where adjustment to change takes place in accordance with the principles of the United Nations; a world where there shall be a permanent state of general and complete disarmament under effective international control and where the resources of nations shall be devoted to man's material, cultural and spiritual advance;

Set forth as the objectives of a program of general and complete disarmament in a peaceful world:

(a) The disbanding of all national armed forces and the prohibition of their reestablishment in any form whatsoever other than those required to preserve internal order and for contributions to a United Nations Peace Force;

(b) The elimination from national arsenals of all armaments, including all weapons of mass destruction and the means for their delivery, other than those required for a United Nations Peace Force and for maintaining internal order;

(c) The establishment and effective operation of an International Disarmament Organization within the framework of the United Nations to ensure compliance at all times with all disarmament obligations;

(d) The institution of effective means for the enforcement of international agreements, for the settlement of disputes, and for the maintenance of peace in accordance with the principles of the United Nations.

Call on the negotiating states:

(a) To develop the outline program set forth below into an agreed plan for general and complete disarmament and to continue their efforts without interruption until the whole program has been achieved;

(b) To this end to seek to attain the widest possible area of agreement at the earliest possible date;

(c) Also to seek — without prejudice to progress on the disarmament program — agreement on those immediate measures that would contribute to the common security of nations and that could facilitate and form a part of that program.

Affirm that disarmament negotiations should be guided by the following principles:

(a) Disarmament shall take place as rapidly as possible until it is completed in stages containing balanced, phased and safe-guarded measures, with each measure and stage to be carried out in an agreed period of time.

(b) Compliance with all disarmament obligations shall be effectively verified from their entry into force. Verification arrangements shall be instituted progressively and in such a manner as to verify not only that agreed limitations or reductions take place but also that retained armed forces and armaments do not exceed agreed levels at any stage.

(c) Disarmament shall take place in a manner that will not affect adversely the security of any state, whether or not a party to an international agreement or treaty.

(d) As states relinquish their arms, the United Nations shall be progressively strengthened in order to improve its capacity to assure international security and the peaceful settlement of differences as well as to facilitate the development of international cooperation in common tasks for the benefit of mankind.

(e) Transition from one stage of disarmament to the next shall take place as soon as all the measures in the preceding stage have been carried out and effective verification is continuing and as soon as the arrangements that have been agreed to be necessary for the next stage have been instituted.

Agree upon the following outline program for achieving general and complete disarmament:

STAGE I

A. *To Establish an International Disarmament Organization:*

(a) An International Disarmament Organization (IDO) shall be established within the framework of the United Nations upon entry into force of the agreement. Its functions shall be expanded progressively as required for the effective verification of the disarmament program.

(b) The IDO shall have: (1) a General Conference of all the parties; (2) a Commission consisting of representatives of all the major powers as permanent members and certain other states on a rotating basis; and (3) an Administrator who will administer the Organization subject to the direction of the Commission and who will have the authority, staff, and finances adequate to assure effective impartial implementation of the functions of the Organization.

(c) The IDO shall: (1) ensure compliance with the obligations undertaken by verifying the execution of measures agreed upon; (2) assist the states in developing the details of agreed further verification and disarmament measures; (3) provide for the establishment of such bodies as may be necessary for working out the details of further measures provided for in the program and for such other expert study groups as may be required to give continuous study to the problems of disarmament; (4) receive reports on the progress of disarmament and verification arrangements and determine the transition from one stage to the next.

B. *To Reduce Armed Forces and Armaments:*

(a) Force levels shall be limited to 2.1 million each for the U.S. and U.S.S.R. and to appropriate levels not exceeding 2.1 million each for all other militarily significant states. Reductions to the agreed levels will proceed by equitable, proportionate, and verified steps.

(b) Levels of armaments of prescribed types shall be reduced by equitable and balanced steps. The reductions shall be accomplished by transfers of armaments to depots supervised by the IDO. When, at specified periods during the Stage I reduction process, the states party to the agreement have agreed that the armaments and armed forces are at prescribed levels, the armaments in depots shall be destroyed or converted to peaceful uses.

(c) The production of agreed types of armaments shall be limited.

(d) A Chemical, Biological, Radiological (CBR) Experts Commission shall be established within the IDO for the purpose of examining and reporting on the feasibility and means for accomplishing the verifiable reduction and eventual elimination of CBR weapons stockpiles and the halting of their production.

C. *To Contain and Reduce the Nuclear Threat:*

(a) States that have not acceded to a treaty effectively prohibiting the testing of nuclear weapons shall do so.

(b) The production of fissionable materials for use in weapons shall be stopped.

(c) Upon the cessation of production of fissionable materials for use in weapons. Agreed initial quantities of fissionable materials from past production shall be transferred to non-weapon purposes.

(d) Any fissionable materials transferred between countries for peaceful uses of nuclear energy shall be subject to appropriate safeguards to be developed in agreement with the IAEA.

(e) States owning nuclear weapons shall not relinquish control of such weapons to any nation not owning them and shall not transmit to any such nation information or material necessary for their manufacture. States not owning nuclear weapons shall not manufacture such weapons, attempt to obtain control of such weapons belonging to other states, or seek or receive information or materials necessary for their manufacture.

(f) A Nuclear Experts Commission consisting of representative of the nuclear states shall be established within the IDO for the purpose of examining and reporting on the feasibility and means for accomplishing the verified reduction and eventual elimination of nuclear weapons stockpiles.

D. To Reduce Strategic Nuclear Weapons Delivery Vehicles:

(a) Strategic nuclear weapons delivery vehicles in specified categories and agreed types of weapons designed to counter such vehicles shall be reduced to agreed levels by equitable and balanced steps. The reduction shall be accomplished in each step by transfers to depots supervised by the IDO of vehicles that are in excess of levels agreed upon for each step. At specified periods during the Stage I reduction process, the vehicles that have been placed under supervision of the IDO shall be destroyed or converted to peaceful uses.

(b) Production of agreed categories of strategic nuclear weapons delivery vehicles and agreed types of weapons designed to counter such vehicles shall be discontinued or limited.

(c) Testing of agreed categories of strategic nuclear weapons delivery vehicles and agreed types of weapons designed to counter such vehicles shall be limited or halted.

E. To Promote the Peaceful Use of Outer Space:

(a) The placing into orbit or stationing in outer space of weapons capable of producing mass destruction shall be prohibited.

(b) States shall give advance notification to participating states and to the IDO of launchings of space vehicles and missiles, together with the track of the vehicle.

F. To Reduce the Risks of War by Accident, Miscalculations, and Surprise Attack:

(a) States shall give advance notification to the participating states and to the IDO of major military movements and maneuvers, on a scale as may be agreed, which might give rise to misinterpretation or cause alarm and induce countermeasures. The notification shall include the geographic areas to be used and the nature, scale and time span of the event

(b) There shall be established observation posts at such locations as major ports, railway centers, motor highways, and air bases to report on concentrations and movements of military forces.

(c) There shall also be established such additional inspection arrangements to reduce the danger of surprise attack as may be agreed.

(d) An international commission shall be established immediately within the IDO to examine and make recommendations on the possibility of further measures to reduce the risks of nuclear war by accident, miscalculation, or failure of communication.

G. To Keep the Peace:

(a) States shall reaffirm their obligations under the U.N. Charter to refrain from the threat or use of any type of armed force — including nuclear, conventional, or CBR — contrary to the principles of the U.N. Charter.

(b) States shall agree to refrain from indirect aggression and subversion against any country.

(c) States shall use all appropriate processes for the peaceful settlement of disputes and shall seek within the United Nations further arrangements for the peaceful settlement of international disputes and for the codification and progressive development of international law.

(d) States shall develop arrangements in Stage I for the establishment in Stage II of a U.N. Peace Force.

(e) A U.N. peace observation group shall be staffed with a

standing cadre of observers who could be dispatched to investigate any situation which might constitute a threat to or breach of the peace.

STAGE II

A. *International Disarmament Organization:*

The powers and responsibilities of the IDO shall be progressively enlarged in order to give it the capabilities to verify the measures undertaken in Stage II.

B. *To Further Reduce Armed Forces and Armaments:*

(a) Levels of forces for the U.S., U.S.S.R., and other militarily significant states shall be further reduced by substantial amounts to agreed levels in equitable and balanced steps.

(b) Levels of armaments of prescribed types shall be further reduced by equitable and balanced steps. The reduction shall be accomplished by transfers of armaments to depots supervised by the IDO. When, at specified periods during the Stage II reduction process, the parties have agreed that the armaments and armed forces are at prescribed levels, the armaments in depots shall be destroyed or converted to peaceful uses.

(c) There shall be further agreed restrictions on the production of armaments.

(d) Agreed military bases and facilities wherever they are located shall be dismantled or converted to peaceful uses.

(e) Depending upon the findings of the Experts Commission on CBR weapons, the production of CBR weapons shall be halted, existing stocks progressively reduced, and the resulting excess quantities destroyed or converted to peaceful uses.

C. *To Further Reduce the Nuclear Threat:*

Stocks of nuclear weapons shall be progressively reduced to the minimum levels which can be agreed upon as a result of the findings of the Nuclear Experts Commission; the resulting excess of fissionable material shall be transferred to peaceful purposes.

D. *To Further Reduce Strategic Nuclear Weapons Delivery Vehicles:*

Further reductions in the stocks of strategic nuclear weapons delivery vehicles and agreed types of weapons designed to counter such vehicles shall be carried out in accordance with the procedure outlined in Stage I.

E. *To Keep the Peace:*

During Stage II, states shall develop further the peace-keeping processes of the United Nations, to the end that the United Nations can effectively in Stage III deter or suppress any threat or use of force in violation of the purposes and principles of the United Nations:

(a) States shall agree upon strengthening the structure, authority, and operation of the United Nations so as to assure that the United Nations will be able effectively to protect states against threats to or breaches of the peace.

(b) The U.N. Peace Force shall be established and progressively strengthened.

(c) States shall also agree upon further improvements and developments in rules of international conduct and in processes for peaceful settlement of disputes and differences.

STAGE III

By the time Stage II has been completed, the confidence produced through a verified disarmament program, the acceptance of rules of peaceful international behavior, and the development of strengthened international peace-keeping processes within the framework of the U.N. should have reached a point where the states of the world can move forward to Stage III. In Stage III progressive controlled disarmament and continuously developing principles and procedures of international law would proceed to a point where no state would have the military power to challenge the progressively strengthened U.N. Peace Force and all international disputes would be settled according to the agreed principles of international conduct.

The progressive steps to be taken during the final phase of the disarmament program would be directed toward the attainment of a world in which:

(a) States would retain only those forces, non-nuclear armaments, and establishments required for the purpose of maintaining internal order; they would also support and provide agreed manpower for a U.N. Peace Force.

(b) The U.N. Peace Force, equipped with agreed types and quantities of armaments, would be fully functioning.

(c) The manufacture of armaments would be prohibited except for those of agreed types and quantities to be used by the U.N. Peace Force and those required to maintain internal order. All other armaments would be destroyed or converted to peaceful purposes.

(d) The peace-keeping capabilities of the United Nations would be sufficiently strong and the obligations of all states under such arrangements sufficiently far-reaching as to assure peace and the just settlement of differences in a disarmed world.

Department of State Publication 7277
Disarmament Series 5
Releases September 1961
Office of Public Services
Bureau of Public Affairs

For sale by the Superintendent of Documents,
U.S. Government Printing Office
Washington 25, D.C.
Price 15 cents

US Government Printing Office - 1961 O–609147

Recommended Reading

This is not intended to be an exhaustive bibliography of all references used in the creation of this book. Instead, it is a recommended reading list, by subject, of the 50-some books I believe to be among the best of the bunch. This is a great place to start your studies.

Liberty as a Concept in Fiction

The Fountainhead. Ayn Rand, The Bobbs-Merrill Company, NY, 1943.
This beautiful novel launched the Philosopher of Freedom onto the world stage. It is uncanny to realize both how brilliant the book is, and how long the problem of collectivism has been plaguing us.

Atlas Shrugged. Ayn Rand, Random House, NY, 1957.
I cannot praise this novel enough. John Galt's 100-page speech on liberty is worth the 1000 pages needed to learn who he is and why he said it.

Nineteen Eighty-Four. George Orwell, New American Library, NY, 1984.
This is the classic book on totalitarianism. Many breathed a sigh of relief when 1984 passed, not having noticed that Orwell's vision had been realized in a more subtle form.

Animal Farm. George Orwell, New American Library, NY, 1964.
"All animals are equal, except some are more equal than others." This brilliant allegory on Communism will trouble and delight.

Brave New World. Aldous Huxley, Sun Dial Press, Garden City, 1932.
We are here introduced to a "kinder-gentler" totalitarian paradise, achieved through the use of drugs, sex, and social planning. When we've mastered genetic engineering, it will be time to look around.

Liberty as a Concept in Non-Fiction

The Law. Frederic Bastiat, trans. Dean Russell, The Foundation for Economic Education, Irvington-on-Hudson, originally published 1850, English translation 1994.
This tiny jewel of a book, some 80 pages, is jam packed with the simplest of ideas, among which is that stealing is wrong, even when done in the name of the state.

The Law Is For All. Aleister Crowley, ed. Louis Wilkinson and Hymenaeus Beta, New Falcon Publications, Tempe, AZ, 1996.
This brilliant analysis of *The Book of the Law* reveals Crowley's fervent embrace of individual rights and Libertarian philosophy. Blows a giant hole through the myth that those who embrace sexual and artistic freedom must also embrace a leftist ideology.

America's Thirty Years War, Who Is Winning? Balint Vazsonyi, Regnery Publishing, Inc, Washington, D.C., 1998.
This pianist, composer, and Hungarian refugee lived as a child under both Naziism and Communism. He came to the U.S. in 1959. A decade later, he noticed that much of the language of the 1960s had a terrifyingly familiar ring. Filled with first hand insights on the nature of tyranny.

From Freedom to Slavery: The Rebirth of Tyranny in America. Gerry Spence, St. Martin's Press, 1993.
The flamboyant, freedom-loving lawyer who defended Randy Weaver — turning a potential death sentence into an acquittal — shares his concerns for America's descent into statism.

Freedom Is a Two-Edged Sword and Other Essays. John Whiteside Parsons, ed. by Cameron and Hymenaeus Beta, Ordo Templi Orientis & New Falcon Publications, New York & Las Vegas, 1989.
The title essay might have been written as a Preface to this book — except it was written before I was born. The other essays may safely be ignored by those so inclined.

THE INTELLECTUAL ROOTS OF AMERICAN LIBERTY

The Debate on the Constitution. 2 vols., selected by Bernard Bailyn, Literary Classics of the United States, Inc., NY, 1977.
This massive two-volume tome provides a wealth of information about the urgency and idealism that accompanied the bold American experiment in Liberty. It catalogs a series of both Federalist and Anti-Federalists speeches, articles, and letters from 1787 to 1788 when the proposed Constitution was being offered to the States for ratification.

The Federalist Papers. ed. Clinton Rossiter, Mentor, NY 1961.
The beauty of this inexpensive paperback, is that for about $7 you can understand the concept of "Original Intent." What did the Founders mean? This book explains it in their own words.

The Anti-Federalist Papers and the Constitutional Debates. ed. Ralph Ketcham, Mentor, NY, 1986.
Hear the dissenters, those who believed the federal system would inevitably tyrannize America. Also includes an excellent selection of the debates during the Constitutional Convention. Your persistence in reading will be infinitely rewarded.

DANGERS FACING MODERN SOCIETY

Death by Government. R. J. Rummel, Transaction Publishers, New Brunswick, 1994.
You'll think twice when you hear, "I'm from the government, and I'm hear to help." Professor Rummel's research is both exacting and frightening.

Lost Rights: The Destruction of American Liberty. James Bovard, second edition, St. Martin's Griffin Edition, NY, 1995.
— *Freedom in Chains: The Rise of the State and the Demise of the Citizen.* St. Martin's Press, NY, 1999
— *Terrorism and Tyranny: Trampling Freedom, Justice, and Peace to Rid the World of Evil.* Palgrave Macmillan, NY, 2003.
These three books each provide exhaustive catalogs of the modern assault on liberty committed in the name of public safety and the rule of the Nanny State. Indispensable for an understanding of the problem.

Paved With Good Intentions: The Failure of Race Relations in Contemporary America. Jared Taylor, Carroll & Graf Publishers, NY, 1992.
A vital and meticulously documented indictment of the racial hypocrisy of modern America, and the demoralizing and divisive effects of political correctness on people of all races.

Treason: Liberal Treachery From the Cold War to the War on Terrorism. Ann Coulter, Crown Forum, NY, 2003.
Why do liberals hate America? She may not have all the answers, but she demonstrates that they do in this well-written, fast-moving, and enjoyable book. If this is the first time you've read the truth of "McCarthyism," you're in for a surprise.

ARCHICTECTS OF THE NEW WORLD ORDER

Tragedy and Hope: A History of the World in Our Time. Carroll Quigley, Angriff Press, Hollywood, originally published 1966, reprinted 1974.
The grand daddy of political conspiracy books. This is the one they all mention, and you'll see why when you wade through its 1300 pages. Quotes in the present book should already have given you an idea of what's here. There's a whole lot more worth reading.

Global Tyranny . . . Step by Step: The United Nations and the Emerging New World Order. William F. Jasper, Western Islands Publishers, Appleton, 1992.
— *The United Nations Exposed: The Internationalist Conspiracy to Rule the World.* The John Birch Society, Appleton, WI, 2001.
Both books document the drive to global government, the history of the movement, and the true consequences of erecting such a leviathan. Jasper exposes globalist plans regarding individual freedom, property rights, criminal justice, finances, child rearing, religion, ecology, and more.

Financial Terrorism: Hijacking America Under the Threat of Bankruptcy. John E. McManus, The John Birch Society, Appleton, 1994.
A sober analysis of the financial dynamics of the plan to weaken America. Examines the International Monetary Fund, the World Bank, and the U.S. Federal Reserve. Explores the consequences of higher taxes, government debt, hidden inflation. and international trade agreements.

Changing Commands: The Betrayal of America's Military. John McManus, The John Birch Society, Appleton, WI, 1995.
Exposes the goal of a supra-national army that will dominate all vestiges of the nation state. A look at the U.S. Constitutional principles being ignored by the strategic alliances and peacekeeping missions into which the U.S. has increasingly allowed itself to be drawn.

The Shadows of Power: The Council on Foreign Relations and the American Decline. James Perloff, Western Islands Publishers, Appleton, 1988.
A superb history of the Council of Foreign Relations (CFR), including its origins, personnel, influence on government and social policies, and ideals.

Philip Dru: Administrator — A Story of Tomorrow (1920–1935). Edward Mandell House, n.p., NY, 1912. (Available from American Opinion Bookstore 1-800-342-6491) This magnum opus of arrogance and hubris is a fictionalized account of the fantasies of a founder of the Council on Foreign Relations. House was also an intimate friend of, and chief advisor to, President Woodrow Wilson.

The Occult Technology of Power. by Peter McAlpine, Loompanics Unlimited, Port Townsend, 1974.
An imaginative account of the intellectual training program for a young leader of the New World Order. It has been called a modern successor to Machiavelli's sixteenth-century classic *The Prince*.

COMMUNISM

Witness. Whittaker Chambers, Random House, NY, 1952.
This is one of the most poignantly written and brilliant books I've read in my life. It is the autobiography of a disillusioned Communist and his embrace of Liberty. I cannot recommend it highly enough. Recently reprinted in paperback by Regnery Publishing.

Radical Son: A Generational Odyssey. David Horowitz, The Free Press, NY, 1997.
Another fascinating autobiography written by a former major theoretician of the New Left. His rejection of its cynical, Communist, anti-freedom agenda should offer a profound warning about modern "Liberalism."

Venona: Decoding Soviet Espionage in America. John Earl Haynes & Harvey Klehr, Yale University Press, New Haven, 1999.
These authors have compiled an excellent series of books on Communism, and the American traitors who worked for Stalin during the Cold War. It's worse than you were taught. McCarthy was actually right.

Perjury: The Hiss-Chambers Case. Allen Weinstein, Random House, NY, 1978, revised 1997.
The author began this book with faith in Hiss's innocence. His research convinced him otherwise (a conclusion he shared with Hiss before the latter's death). The updated edition includes material released during the 1990s with the opening of the Soviet Archives and the Venona cables, which prove Hiss's guilt beyond reasonable doubt.

Joseph McCarthy: Reexamining the Life and Legacy of America's Most Hated Senator. Arthur Herman, The Free Press, NY, 2000.
Although a better book on this controversial anti-Communist remains to be written, this is the best one I've found yet. It unravels the lies and slanders with which this courageous man has been vilified for half a century.

The Black Book of Communism: Crimes, Terror, Repression. ed. Stéphane Courtois, *et. al.*, Harvard University Press, Cambridge, MA, 1999.
850 pages document the brutal atrocities committed in the name of the total state by Communist regimes worldwide during the twentieth-century.

Darkness at Noon. Arthur Koestler, Bantam, Books, NY, 1968.
A fascinating and horrifying fictional account of a Communist Party leader accused of, imprisoned and executed for thought-crimes during the Stalin purges. Written by an ex-Communist who knew of what he spoke.

One Day in the Life of Ivan Denisovich. Aleksandr Solzhenitsyn, trans. by H. T. Willetts, Farrar, Strauss and Giroux, NY, 1991
A brilliantly written (and translated) account of the Stalinist labor camps by the Nobel Prize-winning author who was imprisoned there.

THE SECOND AMENDMENT

To Keep and Bear Arms: The Origins of an Anglo-American Right. Joyce Lee Malcolm, Harvard University Press, Cambridge, 1994.
A scholarly study of the historical roots of the Common Law right to individual self-defense. It provides an accurate examination of the true meaning of, and formative influences upon, the Second Amendment.

Guns and Violence: The English Experience. Joyce Lee Malcolm, Harvard University Press, Cambridge, 2002.
This brilliant follow-up to the book recommended above, compares the availability of personal weapons with the crime rates in British society from the Middle Ages through modern times. History supports the statement that "An armed society is a polite society." Modern British subjects are learning that the converse is also true.

Guns, Crime and Freedom. Wayne LaPierre, Regnery Publishing, Washington D.C., 1994.
— *Guns, Freedom and Terrorism.* WND Books, Nashville, 2003.
Factual presentations of the Second Amendment tradition in America by the primary spokesman for the NRA. Meticulously researched, well-written.

Gun Control, Gateway to Tyranny. Jay Simpkin and Aaron Zelman, Jews for the Preservation of Firearms Ownership, Milwaukee, 1993.
This frightening book presents side-by-side translations of the Nazi Gun Laws of Germany and the 1968 U.S. Gun Control Act, which was directly derived from the Nazi originals.

More Guns, Less Crime: Understanding Crime and Gun Control Laws. John P. Lott, Jr., University of Chicago Press, Chicago, 1998, revised 2000.
An exhaustive analysis of the relationship between crime and weapons in civilian hands, as studied by a celebrated economist and statistician. An armed population is the most effective means of crime control.

Unintended Consequences. John Ross, Accurate Press, St. Louis, 1996.
This is a remarkably creative work for those interested in freedom and American history. It is a treasure trove of gun lore and a great read.

WACO & RUBY RIDGE

Why Waco?: Cults and the Battle for Religious Freedom in America. James D. Tabor and Eugene V. Gallagher, University of California Press, Berkeley, 1995.
A brilliant examination of Waco written by two religious scholars who worked closely with Branch Davidian survivors to understand the dynamics of their faith. Tabor and fellow scholar Phillip Arnold attempted to help end the siege peacefully after David Koresh reached out to them. They were rebuffed by the FBI.

The Ashes of Waco: An Investigation. Dick J. Reavis, Simon & Schuster, NY, 1995.
A detailed review of the entire Waco tragedy, which includes the history and origins of the sect, biographical data on David Koresh and others, and a full accounting of the events up to and including the trial.

Waco: The Rules of Engagement. William Gazicki and Mike McNulty, Somford Entertainment, Video, 1997 (http://www.waco93.com/)
Waco: A New Revelation. Rick Van Fleet and Mike McNulty, MGA Studios, Video, 2000. (http://www.waco-anewrevelation.com/)
These two videos present complete and compelling information on the Waco raid and siege, the Senate hearings that followed the trial, and the disturbing issues I mentioned in my essay. I am told there is a poorly edited version to be avoided, thus please order from the websites noted here.

Ambush at Ruby Ridge: How Government Agents Set Up Randy Weaver and Took His Family Down. Alan W. Bock, Dickens Press, Irvine, CA, 1995.
A sympathetic, accurate and exhaustive account of the Ruby Ridge tragedy, and the trial and acquittal of Randy Weaver, prior to the Senate hearings covered below.

The Federal Siege at Ruby Ridge: In Our Own Words. Randy and Sara Weaver, Ruby Ridge Inc., Marion, MT, 1998.
This heart wrenching personal account also includes an annotated reproduction of the report of the 14 days of hearings on Ruby Ridge conducted in 1995 by the Subcommittee on Terrorism of the Senate Judiciary Committee.

MILITANT ISLAM

What Went Wrong: Western Impact and Middle Eastern Response. Bernard Lewis, Oxford University Press, NY, 2002.
— *The Crisis of Islam: Holy War and Unholy Terror*. Bernard Lewis, The Modern Library, NY, 2003.
Lewis is the pre-eminent living Western scholar on Islam. The first book was written just before September 11, the second soon after. He traces the history of the modern crisis in Islamic culture, and the seductive attraction of the fundamentalist message of hatred.

Holy War, Inc.: Inside the Secret World of Osama bin Laden. Peter L. Bergen, The Free Press, NY, 2001.
Bergen interviewed bin Laden in 1997. His insights into the working of al-Qaeda are first hand and well written. A factual page turner.

American Jihad: The Terrorists Living Among Us. Steven Emerson, The Free Press, NY, 2002.
During his ten years of research into the activities of the modern Islamic terror network in America, Emerson became *persona non grata* in the media because of his politically incorrect findings. After September 11, he was quickly hired as a network consultant.

The Two Faces of Islam: The House of Saud from Tradition to Terror. Steven Schwartz, Doubleday, NY, 2002.
The author is both a Jew and a Sufi with an abiding reverence for Islam. He documents in great detail the Wahhabi fundamentalist agenda, its covert support by the Saudi government, its worldwide reach, and its danger to both Muslims and the West.

The Templars and the Assassins: The Militia of Heaven. James Wasserman, Inner Traditions International, Rochester, VT, 2001.
This book is an excellent reference source for the religious history of Islam, the roots of the historical hatred between Islam and Christianity in the Crusades, and the spiritual creed of the Holy Killer.